Tales from Indochina

To Ralph & Lorraine
with love,

Marilyn

INTERNATIONAL MUSEUM OF CULTURES

PUBLICATION 21

WILLIAM R. MERRIFIELD

Series Editor

DESMOND C. DERBYSHIRE

General Editor

Academic Publications Coordinator

Tales from Indochina

Edited by
Marilyn Gregerson
and Others

INTERNATIONAL MUSEUM
OF CULTURES

Dallas, Texas
1986

© 1986 by the Summer Institute of Linguistics, Inc.

Library of Congress Catalog Card No.: 82-081681

ISBN: 0-88312-169-7

For further information on the cultures of Indochina:

NOTES FROM INDOCHINA on ethnic minority cultures, edited by Marilyn Gregerson and Dorothy Thomas, 1980. $9.45
ISBN: 0-88312-155-7   Microfiche: $6.00

Available at:

The International Museum of Cultures
7500 W. Camp Wisdom Road
Dallas, TX   75236

CONTENTS

CONTENTS

FOREWORD

This volume contains a selection of folktales collected by members of the Summer Institute of Linguistics during fieldwork in Vietnam from 1960 to 1975.

Those of us who were privileged to study the oral literature of the indigenous minorities of Vietnam are deeply grateful to those who have shared this rich tradition with us. Studying the present material in the original languages has contributed to a deeper understanding of each culture through its vocabulary as well as its grammar and discourse style. It is our hope, too, that this published record will contribute towards the preservation of this literature for future generations of the peoples of Indochina.

Many other tales (though often without translation) are available in microfiche from SIL Publications, 7500 West Camp Wisdom Road, Dallas, Texas, 75236.

It is our hope that this collection of folktales will provide the reader with a unique window on cultures whose literatures, despite their richness, are not yet widely known.

Marilyn Gregerson
Dorothy Thomas
Doris Blood
Carol Zylstra

INTRODUCTION

Vietnam's indigenous minority peoples are representatives of several language groupings. Those whose stories are found in this volume are from three language families: Austronesian, Mon-Khmer, and Tai:

Austronesian, Chamic subgrouping:	Cham
	Chru
	Haroi
	Roglai
Mon-Khmer:	
Katuic subgrouping:	Bru
	Pacoh
North Bahnaric subgrouping:	Bahnar
	Cua
	Jeh
	Rengao
	Sedang
South Bahnaric subgrouping:	Chrau
	Mnong
Tai:	Black Tai
	Nung
	Tho
	White Tai

The minority groups whose oral literature was selected for this volume also contrast in their basic forms of social organization as reflected in the tales themselves. The distribution of these societies is as follows:

1) All Austronesian groups in Vietnam, as well as the South Bahnaric Mon-Khmer groups whose territory lies adjacent to Austronesian neighbors, practice matrilineal descent, matrilocal residency, and have matri-sibs. Their homeland is the southern area of

the central highlands (see following map). Thus, the matrilineal groups included in this volume are:

    Austronesian: Cham
                  Haroi
                  Chru
                  Roglai

    Mon-Khmer, South Bahnaric subgrouping: Chrau
                                           Mnong Rlam

It should be noted, however, that the Chrau in some areas are now changing in the direction of the patrilineal emphasis of Vietnamese culture.

2) The North Bahnaric groups of Mon-Khmer represented in this volume all practice bilateral descent and ambilocal residency with the exception of the Cua who live further north contiguous to other patrilineal societies. The bilateral groups whose tales appear in this volume include: Bahnar
                                 Jeh
                                 Rengao
                                 Sedang

3)The Tai language groups along with all of the Katuic groups and the Cua from the North Bahnaric subgrouping of Mon-Khmer practice patrilineal descent, patrilocal residency, and have patri-sibs. The following patrilineal groups are represented in this volume:

    Tai: Black Tai
                              Nung
                              Tho
                              White Tai

    Mon-Khmer:
        Katuic: Bru
                              Pacoh

        South Bahnaric: Cua

The map in figure 3 shows a division of the ethnic groups of the southern part of Vietnam into matrilineal, bilateral, and patrilineal types of social organization.

Customs related to marriage are noticeable in the Rengao story of Bok 'Blar. When the rich man chooses Bok 'Blar for his son-in-law, he does not approach him directly, but asks a go-between to arrange the marriage. In Rengao culture it is possible for either the groom's family or the bride's family to initiate a marriage, but where their economic situation is so disparate, it is appropriate for the obviously more wealthy party to initiate the alliance. Bok 'Blar is acting in a culturally appropriate fashion when he tells the go-between how poor and lazy he is. The custom of in-law avoidance is also strongly portrayed in this story. As in many of the cultures of Vietnam, a Rengao father-in-law or mother-in-law must not speak directly to a son-in-law. Hence, the rich man always sends messages to Bok 'Blar through his daughter. It should also be noted that Bok 'Blar shows respect for his father-in-law by always obeying him regardless of how much he dislikes what he is asked to do.

The custom of ultimogeniture, the favoring of the youngest child in inheritance, is reflected in the fact that the hero or heroine in some of the tales is often the youngest child. Sometimes the hero ends up marrying the youngest daughter of the king or rich man, as in the case of J'Bong Alah, the hero of the Cham tale.

The primary means of subsistence for most of the ethnic groups in this volume is the cultivation of dry rice in swiddens with shifting cultivation, though wet rice cultivation is predominant in the Eastern Cham area and is not uncommon among many other ethnic groups.[2]. Domestic animals include water buffalo, cattle, pigs, goats, and chickens. Some reference is made to domesticated elephants, and some domestic elephants are still found in the southern part of the central highlands.

All of the Mon-Khmer and most of the Austronesian groups have a genre of "Br'er Rabbit"-like folktales about animals who can talk. Many of these stories, which appear in section II, illustrate the triumph of the trickster (the rabbit) over the bully (the tiger). Most of the examples in this volume are from Mon-Khmer languages, though two are from Chru, an Austronesian language.

The hero of the stories in section III is always in some way the antithesis of the ideal man in that society. Though hard work is highly valued, the hero may be extremely lazy, as in the Cua tale, "The Laziest Man in the World," or the Rengao account of "Bok 'Blar." Though a handsome countenance, a muscular body, and clear, light skin are all desired physical characteristics, the hero of these stories may have very dark skin, a pot belly, buck teeth, or otherwise be disfigured, as in the Black Tai story, "Mr. Countless Warts." Alternatively, his body may be covered with a loathsome, itchy, scaly disease, as in the Chrau tale, "Chot Caniet" (**caniet** actually can mean either 'itchy' or 'lazy'). Though courage and bravery are also highly valued in these cultures, the hero of this genre of tales is often a coward. He goes from rags to riches in spite of his shortcomings by means of lies, deceit, and treachery. That is, the "loser" as hero makes it by being "street smart." Part of his reward may, for example, be to marry the daughter of the king or a wealthy man who apparently has no male heirs.

Getting pregnant in a miraculous way is another common motif throughout the area, as in the Black Tai story where the princess becomes pregnant after eating the tangerine that Mr. Countless Warts has rubbed on his body. Another version involves pregnancy through eating or drinking urine, as in the Cua story, "The Laziest Man in the World."

Insofar as religious beliefs are concerned, the traditional religion of the majority of those cultures represented in this volume includes various forms of animism such as beliefs in geographically located spirits. There is a strong belief among Mon-Khmer, Tai, and some of the Austronesian groups concerning the spirit of the rice who is referred to in the Roglai story, "The Great Elephant," which also makes reference to a medicine spirit. Animal sacrifice as a means of placating spirits is common in Austronesian, Tai, and Mon-Khmer groups. The highest sacrifice is that of the water buffalo. However, no reference is made to any kind of animal sacrifice in any of the stories in this volume. The Cham, who ruled Vietnam between the sixth and thirteenth centuries, contrast with other minority groups in their religious orientation. The Eastern Cham are divided into two groups on a religious basis: the first group adhere to Islamic faith, a Chamic form of Islam, while the second group practice an older tradition, a localized form of Brahmanism. These Chamic religious traditions evolved from contact with Hinduism and Islam in earlier centuries. Veneration of the ancestors is part of both traditions. The cult of the ancestors is also important in the Tai groups.

The most feared and powerful animal known to the minority people of Vietnam is the tiger. Though he is the victim of rabbit's tricks in the Tiger and Rabbit stories, he is in reality greatly feared by the people. In the Cham story of "Kam and Hlok," a tiger eats up the wicked half sister, Kam. Connections between tigers and the supernatural are common, and the belief that contemporary living people can voluntarily or involuntarily turn themselves into tigers is widespread. In the Jeh story, "Master Thuan and the Tiger Fairy," for example, a spirit has the capability of transforming itself from a ghost into a beautiful woman and then at will into a man-eating tiger.

Modern-day customs are often confirmed, validated, or explained in these folktales as in others around the world. Rengao informants told us, for example, that in the olden days their forebears would separate the chaff from the rice, only to throw away the rice and eat the chaff. Then one day Grandmother Pom, who, incidentally, they say can still be seen on the face of the moon pounding rice, taught them to throw away the chaff and cook and eat the rice. In the story of "The Monkey Midwife," all Roglai women died after a Caesarean operation to deliver their first-born child. Fortunately, the monkey midwife was finally able to teach them to deliver babies without killing the mother. "The Monkey

Midwife" tale also relates details of "the celebration of the midwife," a ceremony commonly held after the birth of a child.

Transformations of these tales appear, as one might expect, in many other Southeast Asian cultures. For example, versions of "The Youngest Fairy Princess," which we have in the present₃volume from White Tai, are also found in Sabah₄ (Borneo), Malaysia,³ as well as among the Siamese of Thailand.⁴ Interestingly, the White Tai version is much closer to the tale as it is told in Borneo. The White Tai version corresponds with the Sabahan version in that the maiden's wings are stolen, the couple has a child, the wife is from the fairyland above, the husband has many tasks to perform to prove himself worthy of his wife, and a firefly helps him to identify his wife. The Siamese Thai version agrees with the White Tai account in that the maidens were found in a lake in the forest, a ring identifies the husband, and then the wife, child, and husband all return to the earth.

Finally, motifs similar to those in European fairy tales are evident in some of the stories selected here. The Cham tale "Kam and Hlok" has similarities to "Cinderella." In the Cham account a wicked stepmother mistreats Hlok, and her slipper is lost when snatched away by a crow. The king finds the slipper and vows to marry its owner. The Roglai story of "The Great Elephant" is reminiscent of "Hansel and Gretel" in that the children's father repeatedly tries to lose them in the forest at the request of their wicked stepmother.

Marilyn Gregerson

NOTES

1 David D. Thomas and Robert K. Headley, Jr., "More on Mon-Khmer Subgroupings," **Lingua** 25 (1970):398-418, 1970.

2 For detailed information on subsistence techniques see Gerald C. Hickey, 1967. **The Highland People of South Vietnam: Social and Economic Development.** Santa Monica, California: The Rand Corporation.

3 Margaret M. Brooks, **Sabah Folktales** (Kuching, Sarawak: Borneo Literature Bureau, 1960; reprinted, 1970).

4 Margaretta B. Wells, **Thai Fairy Tales** (14 Pramuan Road, Bangkok: Church of Christ in Thailand, 1964).

THE LEGEND OF KAM AND HLOK

This story in Eastern Cham was told by the father of L.,
about fifty years old and was translated by David Blood.

Kam and Hlok were sisters who had the same father but different
mothers. When Hlok was still very small, her mother died. Later,
her father remarried and her half sister Kam was born.

One day Kam and Hlok went fishing. Hlok caught a lot of fish,
but Kam just caught a few. On their way home, they passed under a
tamarind tree. Kam said, "You climb up and pick some tamarinds to
take home for soup. I'll stay down here and watch the fish."

Hlok agreed and climbed the tree. While she was picking tamarinds, her half sister poured all of the fish into her own basket
and ran home. She lied to her mother, saying, "Hlok didn't get any
fish, and she's still dawdling along on her way home."

Hlok had seen Kam pour out her basket of fish, so when she
returned to the basket she was surprised to see one small fish
still inside: a small **charok**. Hlok carried her fish home and put
it in the well at the back of the house. From then on at each meal
she would save a half bowl of rice for the fish, and after doing
the dishes, she would take the rice out and call, "Charok!, come
on and eat your rice." The fish then swam to the surface to
receive its meal.

One day Kam discovered what Hlok was doing and told her mother
about it. So Kam's mother went to the well and called the fish,
just as Hlok did. The fish that answered the summons had by now
grown to the size of a person's thigh.

When the fish came up to the surface, Kam's mother scooped it
out and cut off its head. Later she cooked it and ate it.

That day when Hlok came home from tending the goats and had had
something to eat, she went out as usual to the well and called the
fish. But no fish came. Hlok was very sad.

1

That night a woman appeared to Hlok in a dream and said, "Your fish has already become food for Kam's mother, and its bones are buried at the back of the kitchen. But," promised the woman, "if you will dig up the bones and bury them beneath your bed, something wonderful will appear."

Early the next morning Hlok arose and went out to the back of the kitchen, where she found the bones just as the woman had said. She dug them up and buried all of them under her bed, according to the instructions of the woman in her dream.

A month later, Hlok dug under the bed and found a lovely pair of slippers where the fish bones had been. The slippers were embroidered with gold thread: they were indeed very beautiful. Hlok was delighted.

After that, even when she went to tend goats, Hlok would wrap up the slippers and take them with her. But one day when she went down to bathe in the stream, she left the shoes on the bank. A crow flew by and snatched up one of them and flew away with it. Hlok was deeply grieved by the loss, and from then on never risked taking the remaining slipper with her.

Not long afterward, the king and his men were out hunting when they came upon a very beautiful shoe. The king stared at the shoe for some time and fell in love with the unknown owner. He decreed that whoever owned this exquisite shoe would become the next queen. He sent a letter throughout the kingdom and neighboring countries to search out the beautiful young girl whose foot would fit the shoe that he'd found. Parents everywhere brought their beautiful daughters to the palace in high hopes that one of them would become queen.

Kam's mother, hearing about the king's decree and being very ambitious for her daughter, dressed Kam in the finest clothes, bracelets and rings, and sent her to the palace. Hlok begged permission to go with Kam to watch the proceedings, but her step-mother said, "No." Instead, she gave Hlok a lot of busywork. She got a basket of rice, a basket of beans, and a bowl of sesame and poured them all together. Then she ordered Hlok to separate them all again. When this was done, she said Hlok could go to the palace.

Hlok wanted desperately to see the king's palace so she worked very hard, trying to separate the rice, beans, and sesame. But, after working from dawn to sunset, she had only separated out one small bowl of rice. Exhausted, she went to sleep. Seeing poor Hlok and the injustice of her stepmother, God had compassion and sent down sparrows and pigeons to finish the sorting. When Hlok awoke and saw that all the work had been done, she was very grateful to God for his help.

After taking the sorted grains back to her astonished step-mother, Hlok excused herself, hurriedly bathed, and dressed in her best clothes. Then, taking the one shoe with her, she set off for the palace.

As she approached the palace gates, she met many young maidens from wealthy homes who had been turned away because they could not wear the shoe. Hlok went on and soon was ushered into the palace. The servants presented the shoe, Hlok slipped it on, and it fit perfectly. One of the messengers ran to tell the king: "Hlok's foot fits the shoe!"

The king was overjoyed. Immediately he sent for Hlok to join him in the throne room. Then the king proclaimed a thirty-day wedding celebration--enough time to give everyone a chance to come, even those from faraway countries. When the news came to Kam and her mother, they were overcome with jealousy and anger. They were so angry they wanted to kill Hlok.

One day after she had been queen for some time, Hlok made a return visit to her native village to see her father, stepmother and younger sister. Kam and her mother, still filled with hate, saw Hlok coming. But when she arrived, they pretended to be glad to see her. After they had talked together awhile, Kam invited Hlok out to the garden. She pointed up to a cluster of betel nut and remarked, "Mother likes so much to chew fresh betel; it's a pity I can't climb up to pick it for her."

But Hlok replied, "I'll do it." So she took off her outside clothing and shoes and climbed up the betel nut tree. Kam waited until Hlok had climbed all the way to the top. Then she took hold of the tree and shook it violently, not paying any attention to Hlok's pleas to stop. At last Hlok could hold on no longer: she fell from the top of the tree and was killed.

After Kam and her mother had dug a hole and buried Hlok, they dressed Kam in Hlok's clothes. Since Kam and Hlok looked just alike, Kam passed easily for her half sister, the rightful queen. The king soon noticed a difference in his heretofore sweet-tempered queen, but he didn't say anything. Instead, to soothe his aching heart he spent as much time outside of the palace as he could. Everyday he went hunting with his men.

Meanwhile, over Hlok's grave there sprang up an ebony (or **kĭa**) tree, and it produced a fruit as large as a bowl. A poor old childless woman passed by, carrying a basket on her head. As she stopped to rest her burden under the tree, she looked up and saw this large persimmon-like fruit, almost ripe. She very much wanted it, but was afraid to pick it.

"How nice it would be," she thought, "if that fruit would fall down into my basket."

No sooner had the thought taken form in her head than ker-plunk! The fruit fell down straight into her basket. Delighted, the woman carried her new treasure home. There she examined the fruit carefully, feeling it gently and inhaling its sweet aroma, but she didn't dare eat it. She decided to hide it in the rice storage pot.

When she awoke the next morning, the woman was surprised to see a tray of rice and a pot of tea. She puzzled over this, not knowing quite what to make of it. She hesitated, staring at the delicious-looking food, half wanting to eat it and half afraid to. Finally, she tasted a little. It was the most delicious food she had ever eaten! After she had eaten her fill, she felt very content.

That night the old woman continued to wonder where the food had come from. She went to bed, but she didn't sleep. She stayed awake, quietly watching. About the time the cock crows, she saw a very beautiful girl come out of the rice storage pot, go into the kitchen, and light a fire to heat water and make rice.

The woman crawled out of bed and sneaked over to the rice storage pot. She saw that the ebony fruit was now nothing but two hollow halves: only the peeling remained. The woman thought a minute, then took the peelings and hid them.

The girl finished cooking and returned to the storage pot, but her fruit "skin" was gone! Then the woman ran out to her and hugged her, saying, "Oh granddaughter, please stay with me. I need you." From then on, "Aunt Ebony" (as the old woman called the girl) stayed with the old woman, and the two took care of each other.

One day the king and his men were out hunting, but they became very thirsty by midmorning and turned into the old woman's house for a drink. When Aunt Ebony peeked out and recognized the king, she folded a betel chew in a special way and asked the old woman to present it to him.

When the king saw the betel chew, he was reminded of his wife Hlok. "Who folded this betel?" he asked.

The woman replied, "My foster granddaughter did it."

"Please let me meet her," the king requested.

When the king saw that Aunt Ebony looked exactly like his wife, he asked her some pertinent questions. Aunt Ebony told the king everything.

The reunited husband and wife embraced each other and cried. The king then asked the old woman if she would let his wife go again to live in the palace. She consented.

The king went on ahead to the palace, drove Kam out of his house, and ordered his men to fetch litters to bring Queen Ebony and her foster grandmother to the palace, where they had a joyful feast for the whole country.

As for Kam, halfway down the road from the palace, she met a tiger which struck her down and tore her to pieces. Kam's mother, upon hearing the news, was overcome with grief, fell ill, and followed her daughter in death.

This story shows that whoever lives right will be rewarded, but those with bad hearts will come to a bitter end and suffer the destruction of their offspring.

THE YOUNGEST FAIRY PRINCESS

This story was told in White Tai by P.
and was translated by Jean Donaldson.

Once upon a time there lived a poor man in the hut he had built at the edge of a forest beside a large lake. His parents were dead and he had no relatives. He managed to make a poor living by cutting firewood in the forest and selling it.

One morning at the lake, he chanced to see seven fairy princesses descend from the sky and land on the shore. He saw them take off their wings and their clothes and run into the lake for a swim. The man stayed carefully hidden, watching the princesses swim happily together, unaware that anyone else was near.

The man thought to himself: "I wonder what would happen if I took a pair of their wings and hid it?" Stealthily, he crept over, grabbed a pair of wings, and ran away.

When the princesses finished bathing, they got dressed, donned their wings, and flew away, all except the youngest fairy princess, who couldn't leave because she couldn't find her wings. She became more and more distressed as she searched and searched, but couldn't find them. Despairing, she sat down and cried. Evening fell. She became cold and frightened, not knowing where to go or what to do. Suddenly, she saw a light in a hut at the edge of the forest, went over to it, and saw the poor man.

"Have you seen my wings?" she inquired of the man. "I'm the youngest of seven fairy princesses who came down together to swim in the lake. And now all the others have gone home, but I can't leave until I find my wings. Someone took them; I don't know who. Please help me."

"I'm sorry, but I haven't seen your wings," the man replied. "I live all alone in this poor hut. You're welcome to stay with me if you like."

Not knowing what else to do, the princess agreed to stay. After some time, the princess and the man decided to get married, and a year later their first child was born.

6

As the child grew and was able to sit up, the mother left him occasionally in the care of his father while she went out on errands. Whenever the child fussed or cried, his father gave him the fairy wings to play with, and the boy was content.

One day when the boy was old enough to talk, and his father was out gathering firewood, the child began to cry, and nothing his mother did would soothe him. He kept sobbing, "Me wan wins," and pointed toward the storehouse.

Puzzled, his mother went to investigate. How surprised she was to find her pair of long lost wings in the rice storehouse! The princess was overjoyed. She tried them out immediately, flying about outside the hut. Then she put the wings back exactly where they had been before. But thereafter, whenever her husband was away, the princess got out her wings and practiced while her baby watched.

One day when the child was old enough to walk and his father was away, the princess took out her wings and called her child over to her. "Good-bye, darling! Mother must return to the sky country now. You stay here with Daddy! If you miss me, then you and Daddy must come together to find me."

With that, she took off her ring and gave it to the child. Then she put on her wings and flew away. Watching her go, the little boy began to cry. He was still crying when his father returned. When he found out that his wife had gone and had left only her ring behind, the man, too, was grief-stricken. Father and child clung together, weeping over the loss of the princess.

As the days wore on, the man missed his wife more and more so that at last he determined to look for her. He set off with his son on his back and walked and walked, but he didn't really have any clear idea of where he was going or the best way to get there.

Once he fell into a small opening in the ground in the forest. He managed to get out and walked on, asking every bird and animal he met the whereabouts of the young princess. But no one knew.

One day the man came to a thick part of the forest where a large rock was right in the middle of the path, noisily chewing its cud. The man and his son were not able to get by. A fox came along and said, "Pick some fruit and throw it into the rock. He will chew it until his teeth become sensitive, then he'll open his mouth, then you can slip through." So the man picked some fruit nearby, dropped it in the rock for it to chew, and waited for its teeth to become sensitive. Then the rock opened its mouth. The father picked up his child hurriedly and crawled past to the other side.

So the two of them, father and child, continued on and on, enduring many hardships, until one day they reached a river with nine so-called "iron branches." Even iron dissolved in this river, so people could not wade or swim across it.

Discouraged after their long journey, the father and his son sat on the edge of the river and cried. Then along came a dog with nine heads and nine tails. "What's the matter?" he asked.

"We've come to look for the young princess who lives in the sky country," the man replied, "but I don't see how we can get there, since we can't cross the river."

"I will take you across on one condition," said the dog--"that you don't laugh while we're in the middle of the river."

The man and his son agreed and climbed onto the dog's back. But when they were crossing the first branch, the dog made a strange sound, so that the man couldn't stifle a chuckle. As soon as he did so, one of the heads and one of the tails fell off the dog. He was left with only eight of each.

Before crossing the next branch, the dog again commanded, "Don't laugh!" But as they crossed that branch and each successive one, the man heard the funny noise, and each time he couldn't help laughing. After they had crossed eight of the nine branches of the river, the dog had lost eight heads and eight tails. He had only one of each left, and there was still one branch left to cross.

"Whatever happens," the dog warned, "this time you must not laugh. If you do, we'll all die."

So the man took a cloth and tied it over his mouth, and thus the child, father, and dog arrived safely on the other side of the river. In olden times, all dogs had nine heads and nine tails, but eight of each had come off during this dog's travel across the river and that is why today dogs have only one head and one tail.

Father and child continued on their journey. It began to get dark, and they were still looking for a place to stop and rest when they met a phoenix.

"Can you tell us the way to sky country?" they asked.

The phoenix replied, "It's a very long way. You couldn't possibly get there today. But I'm going there tomorrow to take part in the celebration of the young princess's return from earth. If you would like to come along, then sleep here under my wings tonight. Tomorrow you may accompany my mother and me to sky country."

In the morning, the mother phoenix came for her child, and all four of them flew to the sky country. She carried the man and the boy as far as the river that borders sky country. As they climbed down from her wing, they thanked her very much for her help, and walked on toward the village.

In the village they saw some servant girls drawing water. "Do you know where the youngest princess lives?" the man inquired of them.

But the girls only laughed. "Oh ho! As dirty and ugly as you are, asking for the princess, indeed! How ridiculous! We're here drawing water for her bath," they added importantly. "The princess has only just returned from earth, and there's going to be a celebration." With that, they turned abruptly and walked away.

The man followed them, pleading, "We've walked a long way; we're very tired and thirsty. Please, could you give us a drink?"

One of the maids then let down her bamboo water container for them to drink from. The man slipped off the princess's ring and dropped it in the water container when the maids weren't looking. Then the father and boy went on their way to beg food at the home of an old widow at the edge of town.

Meanwhile, the maids returned to the palace and emptied out the water containers into the tub for the princess's bath. During her bath, the princess noticed a shiny object in the water. She took it out and immediately recognized it as the ring she had left behind with her son. "How did it come to be here?" she wondered.

She called her maids to ask, "Did you see anything strange at the river today?"

One of the maids answered: "We didn't notice anything strange. All we saw was a boy and a poor, dirty, ugly man who asked us for a drink."

Then the princess knew for certain that it was her husband and son who had come to look for her. She sent someone straight off to find them and bring them to the palace. Soon a servant found them resting at the widow's house. "Come quickly!" he urged. "The princess wants to see you!"

When they arrived at the palace, the princess went and told the king all that had happened on earth and how her husband and son had journeyed all the way from earth to sky country in search of her.

The king replied, "Fine. But if he wants to be my son-in-law, he must first pass the three tests I will give him. If he is successful, I will give you to him in marriage according to the custom of the sky country."

Now the king owned three thousand buffalo, each with its own hitching post. The first task he gave to the man was to tie each of the buffalo to its own post. If he made even one mistake, the princess was lost to him forever.

The poor man sat for a time, bewildered. Then, filled with despair at the impossiblity of the task, he began to weep. When evening came, a firefly happened along and asked, "Why are you crying?" So the man told him about the impossible task the king had given to him.

"Don't worry," the firefly assured him. "Just follow me, and I'll show you what to do. When I light on a buffalo and fly over to a post, you tie the buffalo to that post."

The man and the firefly set to work, and just before daybreak, the last buffalo was tied to his post. That day, the king arrived, and he was very pleased when he saw all the buffalo tied correctly.

"Well done," he said. "Your next task will be to sow this sack of grain on the plowed field on the outskirts of town. After you have sown it, you must pick up every single seed again."

The man took the seed and began to sow the field. Sowing was easy, but he didn't know how he could possibly pick up every seed again. As he cried out in frustration, a bird came along. After he listened to the man explain the problem, the bird said, "Don't worry. Everything is going to be all right. My friends and I will pick up all the seeds." The bird called, and several thousand birds came to pick up the grain in the field. But because they were tired and hungry, the birds ate a few of the seeds as they went along.

The king noticed that some of the seed was missing and went back to inquire of the man what had happened.

"Well," the man confessed, "this much is here thanks to the birds who helped pick it up. But they were very hungry so they ate a little."

The king was very angry. He called the birds to come and then he twisted their necks to get the grain back. That is why to this day that kind of bird has a crop in the upper part of the neck and not below the neck like other birds.

Then the king summoned the man and gave him one final command. "When night comes, you must search for the princess's room. If you have not found it by dawn you cannot marry her."

This news upset the man more than ever. The king's palace contained 100,000 rooms, and how was he ever to find the right one?

When night fell, however, along came a rat and said, "Just follow me. When I slip this dried leaf under the door, that is the room where you will find the princess."

The man followed along obediently. At midnight when they were only half way through the house, a cat suddenly jumped out, grabbed the rat, and ate it.

The man was left alone, not knowing which way to turn. Discouraged, he sat down and cried. Then a firefly came to his aid once more. "Just follow me. The door I light on will be the princess's."

All this time the princess was waiting in her room. She had been worrying, too, anxious lest the tasks proved too difficult for her husband. She wondered if he would be able to find her in time, and worried that she might never see him again.

On and on, up and up the staircases trudged the man behind the firefly. Through all of the passages of the house they walked until almost daylight. Finally, the firefly alighted upon a door. The man knocked, and the door opened. There was the princess! How happy they were to be together again! They danced round and round, clinging to each other and crying for joy.

When the king arrived and saw the man and the princess together, he was very pleased. A great wedding feast was prepared and they were married once more, this time according to the laws of sky country.

Some time later the king let them go back to earth. And there the man ruled as a king until he was very old.

THE STORY OF THE WING-WONG VULTURES

This story was told in Bahnar by Mr. B. a young man of
eighteen and was translated by John and Betty Banker.

Long ago in the land of Grandfather Roh, there lived two Wing-Wong vultures--a male and his mate. These vultures were hated and feared by the people of the villages in that area because they had eaten thousands of village people.

Finally, the people of Grandfather Roh's village met together to decide how to get rid of the vultures.

One man said, "The Wing-Wong vultures come to earth when they smell hog roasting or hear the large gongs being played."

Grandfather Roh said to him, "Do you really know if this is true or not?"

"Yes," the man replied, "I know it is true. A man from another place told me of the tragedy in his village because the vultures were attracted to that area."

Grandfather Roh was skeptical, and he told the man he would roast a hog to see if the vultures would come down. "Don't do it!" the man protested. "The vultures will come and eat all the people of our village."

Grandfather Roh would not listen but went ahead and roasted the hog. When the aroma of cooking pork reached the vultures, the husband remarked, "Hmmm. Wife, I smell the hog roasting down there in the village. It is calling me very strongly to go down there. But first you must divine by handspans to see if I should go."

The wife divined by handspans but received a negative divination. However, she counseled, "You go down anyway. It won't be hard for you to eat them."

The hungry male vulture left immediately for the village. As he descended, his mighty wings covered the sun, and all became as dark as night. The villagers ran to their houses.

The vulture landed in a large tree on the outside of town. Readily giving way to such a weighty burden, the tree began to sway back and forth. The villagers were terrified. "If that tree, large as it is, sways back and forth like a young sapling, think what the vulture could do to us!"

But Grandfather Roh urged, "Come on! We must catch this vulture and kill him!"

His pleas fell on deaf ears. That day the vulture ate more than a hundred people.

After he had eaten his fill and flown away, the villagers were more frightened than ever. Some wanted to run away; others were very angry at Grandfather Roh and blamed him for the disaster. Many felt that he should pay damages to the families who had lost relatives to the vulture.

Grandfather Roh carefully considered the matter, then called the whole village together. "I want to talk to you all for a little while," he announced, "because I have been thinking very hard about our village's survival and I believe I have the answer. This is my proposal: None of you should run away, because together we can fight and defeat the vulture. Everyone in the village must sharpen stakes and place them points upward all around the large tree. When the vulture comes back, he's sure to land there again and we'll kill him."

All those villagers who did not accept Grandfather Roh's plan fled to other villages. Everyone else did as he suggested. When the stakes were in place, Rok and Set and their two servants, the nighthawk and the fox, began making a long-handled hook to be used to pull down the vulture from the tree. The nighthawk did the welding for the hook while the fox worked the bellows. Rok and Set helped by welding more and more pieces on the handle. Soon it was long enough to reach to the very top of the tree.

Seeing that the hook and stakes were at last in readiness, Grandfather Roh called all of the villagers to gather around the tree. They made a fire once more at the base of the tree and began to roast the pig. Once more Grandfather Roh beat the large gongs, so loudly that they could be heard all over the earth and sky. When they heard the gongs, many people from neighboring villages came to help kill the vulture.

Meanwhile, the delicious aroma of the roasting hog again wafted up to the vulture. "Wife," he said, "my nose smells pork. I'd like to go down and eat some more of those show-off people, acting like heroes and mandarins! Watch me go down and finish them off! But, first, you must divine for me to see if this venture will turn out well."

As the vulture wife was about to carry out his request, he sneezed (which was a bad omen). "There!" she said, "that proves they are stronger than you are." The divination confirmed this negative assessment, but the vulture refused to believe it. And so he started down toward the village. Again his wings shut out the light from the sun and the sky darkened as if night were drawing near.

Grandfather Roh and his followers, waiting at the foot of the tree, encouraged one another, saying, "Let's not be afraid. We're brave. Why should we fear him?" All together, they gave a loud shout, hoping to scare the vulture. Then, as they remembered all of the people he had eaten, they renewed their determination to kill him. They vowed to give the effort everything they had.

Then the vulture was upon them, swooping down from the sky, his massive body darkening the horizon. As he landed on the tree, he flapped his wings and all the people fell down, tumbling over one another.

Rok and Set, however, managed to hook the vulture's neck, and with all their might they tried to pull him down. But the vulture was so strong in clinging to the tree that the hook straightened out. So the vulture freed himself and returned to his home in the sky.

Grandfather Roh thought things out again. Then he appointed someone to climb up the tree and cut a notch in the branch that the vulture had landed on. The branch would thus be weakened and easily break under the vulture's tremendous weight. The next day everyone gathered to discuss the problem once more.

"Those who have crossbows or swords or spears and shields must all meet at the tree again," Grandfather Roh told them. "When the vulture comes, everyone attack!"

This time everyone was agreeable to his plan. They fell into talking about how things had gone when the vulture came the last time. "This time," Grandfather Roh admonished, "our hook must be strong enough."

Then all of them began to argue over who should make the hook. Each one wanted to help because of the anger and hatred they felt toward the vulture for eating their families. Those who had lost children said they wanted to spear the vulture in the eye or eat its nose.

Some time after this, they were ready to try again. They roasted a hog and beat the large gongs. Once again the vultures were attracted to earth. The vulture wife remarked to her husband, "Those people are still alive, husband."

"Do another divination," he replied, "to see if I will have success if I go."

Again the divination was negative, but the husband vulture decided to go anyway. Once on his way, he sneezed, but he ignored the bad omen and kept going. Down, down came the vulture, darkening the sky as he approached the village.

Grandfather Roh and the villagers were ready for him. "Look! There he comes!" the people cried.

"Oh I would love to eat him!" many said. "Even though his body is so evil-looking, I'd love to eat him! And it's not going to be hard. Just watch!" others declared.

The vulture landed on the tree as before. Then Set and Rok worked fast to hook him securely--Rok hooked him around his neck, Set around his feet. Everyone pulled, but the vulture didn't budge. They pulled again, with no success.

Someone suggested, "Let's pull one more time and give it all we've got."

They pulled until the sweat was pouring off their bodies. The longer they pulled, the harder they pulled. Finally, crack! The branch broke and the mighty vulture fell to the ground. Quickly, people tied him fast--some tied his wings, some tied his feet, while Rok and Set tied the hook to the tree.

Then Rok and Set demanded of the vulture, "Cough up our friends!" The vulture refused.

"Give them back," the villagers insisted. "You've eaten thousands of people. If you don't vomit them up, we'll kill you."

Then some people began piling dry bamboo, grass, and dead trees over the vulture's body, threatening to burn him, but the vulture didn't give in. Rok also continued talking to the vulture, trying to persuade him to vomit the people, but the vulture remained obstinate.

"Since he doesn't agree," the villagers said, "Let's kill him and be done with it. If we let him live, he'll always be a threat to us."

The vulture feared for his life, so he began to vomit people. He vomited up piles and piles of people. After drying them off and counting them, the villagers discovered that there were more than a thousand. But even so, some people were missing.

"Vomit again!" they demanded. But the vulture refused.

So everyone fell on him, stabbing and spearing him and shooting him with crossbows. When the vulture was near death, Rok said, "Give us back the rest of the people you've eaten."

"I won't," said the vulture. So the people stabbed him again.

"Will you eat anymore of us if we let you live?" asked Rok.

"Yes," answered the vulture.

So the villagers set fire to the dry bamboo, grass, and wood. Soon all of the vuture's feathers were burned off.

Again Rok asked, "Are you still determined to eat us?"

"I am," replied the vulture.

At this point Rok felt that it would be hopeless to try to reason further with the vulture.

"Let's loosen the hooks and untie the vulture," he said.

"But," the villagers objected, "he'll get free!"

"He can't get away," Rok assured them, "because he can't fly. The fire has eaten away his wings and tail."

When they had untied him, everyone began chopping away at him, cutting his thighs and legs to bits. Some cooked and ate the bits they had cut off. Others just threw the pieces all over the ground. When they were sure they had killed him, Rok proclaimed, "The victory is ours!"

But just a little later they were stunned as they watched the vulture bring back his flesh and become whole as he was before. The villagers were distraught, not knowing what to do.

"Let's cut him up into very small pieces as we did before," directed Rok. "Only this time, let's throw the pieces into the river. Maybe then he will not be able to come back to life."

But before they cut him up, the people gave the vulture one last chance. "Are you determined to keep on eating us if we let you go?" they asked.

"I am resolved to do so," replied the vulture.

So they cut him again into small pieces and threw all the pieces into the river. Just as the vulture flesh was about to come together again as a body, a school of fish came and gobbled up the pieces.

And so the Wing-Wong vulture died.

But the bits of flesh that fell onto the ground or were not eaten by the fish in the water changed into mosquitoes--the large kind that still bite us today. Yes, those mosquitoes originally came from the flesh of the Wing-Wong vulture.

GREAT ELEPHANT

This story was told in Roglai by Mr. A. H., about forty
years old, and was translated by Vurnell Cobbey.

Once upon a time Great Elephant lived on the earth. Her husband
was a human being, and they had two sons. One day Great Elephant
died, and afterwards the father took a new wife whose name was
Dararint. Dararint already had one daughter, and she hated the
children of Great Elephant very much.

Every day the two boys played with sesame flowers. Whenever
Dararint saw them doing this, she would pretend to be sick. So she
slept every day and never did any work.

One day when her husband came back from the forest, she greeted
him with, "Oh, I'm so sick. What can I do? My illness is caused by
those children playing with sesame flowers, which offends the
medicine spirit and the rice spirit. People are saying that their
father should take them away. I'm sure if you do that, I'll feel
much better tomorrow."

So the next day the father took all three children to the
woods, intending to leave them there. After they had walked a
while, the father asked, "Children, do you know your way in this
part of the woods?"

And the children replied, "Yes, father."

So the father took them further and further into the woods,
until at last when he asked them if they knew their way, they
answered, "No father, we don't." And there he left them and went
home. His wife was pleased.

But that afternoon the three children found their way back home
from the woods. When Dararint saw them, she again feigned
sickness. "Why did you leave them where they could find their way
back? Here I am sick, so what can I do about it? Now go back and
lose them for good."

The next morning, the father took the three children to the
forest again with the same intention of losing them. After they

17

had walked a while, he said to one of the children, "Child, do you know your way in that dark forest over there?"

"No, father, I don't," the child replied.

So the father left them there. Then seeing a parrot, the father said, "Parrot, if my children call soon, you answer, all right?"

Then he called to his children, "Children, you stay here. I'm just going off a little ways. If you call and I answer sweetly, then come. But if I answer roughly, then wait ... wait until I answer sweetly before coming." Then the father went to defecate and went on home.

In a little while, the children called out, "Father, we're lost. Can we come?"

The parrot answered sweetly, so the children went as instructed. Then they smelled where their father had defecated and realized that he had gone again.

"Oh dear, our father has left us!" they cried in despair.

By now it was late afternoon, so the three children looked for a place to sleep. The two children of Great Elephant asked Dararint's child, "Do you want to sleep on the ground or on the rock?"

"I wouldn't think of sleeping on the ground. There are worms. I'll sleep on the rock."

So she slept up on the rock while the two children of Great Elephant slept on the ground. The next morning when the boys awoke, they found Dararint's daughter dead from worms which had entered her. What should they do now? they wondered.

Then Great Elephant spoke to them in a dream: "You two must roast the child of Dararint there. I'll cut firewood to help you." So their mother brought firewood. But some of the wood was still green, so the children wondered aloud, "Now how are we going to start a fire?"

That night when the two children were asleep together, the younger brother awoke and said, "Oh, brother, brother, look! I see something just like a fire!"

"What fire could there be here?" replied the older brother. "This is the forest of our father, the area of our mother. During the day we can look for fire, but since it's night, you're only dreaming."

But the younger brother persisted. "There is a fire. Come and see."

So the older one got up and saw that there really was a fire. Then they slept a little longer, before the younger brother once more aroused. "The potatoes are making me itch!" he said.

"What potatoes are there here?" retorted his brother.

"Get up and see."

So he got up and saw that there were indeed potatoes around them. Then their mother, Great Elephant, told them in a dream that they could eat all of the potatoes around--all of the potatoes on both sides of the main root, that is, but to leave the main root alone.

They slept again for a short while, and again the younger brother awoke, this time seeing a knife.

"Brother, brother," he cried, "I feel just like I've been hurt by a very sharp knife."

"What knife is there here?" scoffed his brother. "Look in the daytime and sleep at night."

"Get up and see for yourself," replied the other.

So the brother got up and saw that what his younger brother had said was true.

The next morning, the boys started a fire, roasted the potatoes, and ate them. When they had finished eating, they made a fire to roast Dararint's daughter. The delicious aroma of roasting flesh attracted all of the four-footed animals. Suddenly, Great Elephant fell down on her knees with a thud. At this noise, the wild pigs, deer, elephants, rhinoceros, carabao, and buffalo all came running. They ran, pushed, shoved, and trampled each other until they all died in the stampede. So the two children went out and took the meat from these animals, singed it, and dried it over the fire in order to be able to eat some later.

Then they set off to clear a field. They started hacking down a large vine, cutting a little on it every day. On the seventh day, it came apart and fell down together with bamboo and other trees. As a whole section of the forest was falling, the brothers said, "Okay, that's enough. This is plenty of land for us to plant."

Not having any seed to plant, the boys decided to leave the field until it was dry enough to burn. When the time came, the fire scorched the earth and cleared the land. Then they made a bow and shot a pigeon. They cut open its crop and recovered seeds of corn, rice, vegetables, and melons. These they planted at the center of the field.

After a while, the seeds sprouted, and a grasshopper came to eat. "Hey, who's eating here? This field belongs to orphans."

"Don't chase me away," the grasshopper replied. "If you let me eat until I'm satisfied, I'll fly over your field and cause it to sprout many plants." So the brothers consented.

When the grasshopper had finished eating, he did as he had promised, and the rice yield increased. Then the two children went to look for rattan to make a shelter to watch for pigeons. Also they set a trap and caught a turtle, intending to eat it. But the turtle, speaking in their own language, said, "Don't eat me. Let me keep watch over your field." So the boys agreed not to eat the turtle in exchange for his watching the field. Every morning, the turtle walked around watching the field.

Each day was the same until one day the turtle saw an elephant come to the upper part of the field. Moving to the center of the field, he saw that the elephant had trampled down all of the rice. As he saw the elephant turn away, he called, "Hey, you! What are you doing here? You've ruined all this rice which belongs to poor orphans. Drop your tusk off here."

So the elephant shook until his right tusk came off, and he went away. The turtle returned to the house and told the two brothers what had happened. When the boys went out to inspect the field, they saw that everything the turtle had told them was true.

They returned to the field with a large cloth to carry the tusk home. Then they heard the voices of people laughing at them.

"Why are you laughing at us? Just to make us feel bad?" They carried the tusk home and put it up on the drying rack. But the turtle advised, "Don't leave it in the center of the house. Put it in a corner." So the brothers complied; then they went out to the field again.

The tusk was left in the corner, in the drying rack over the fire. While the brothers were gone, people from inside the tusk came out and urinated in the fireplace, putting out the fire. Returning from the field, the brothers found that the fire had gone out. Without fire, how could they eat? they wondered.

But then, looking up at the center of the house, they saw an abundance of fish, dried meat, roasted meat, and lovely white rice. They wondered if they should eat it. But the older brother said, "Whether we die from it or not, let's eat!"

As soon as they had eaten, the older brother went back to the field, but the younger brother remained in the house, hiding. All of a sudden two people came out of the tusk. They were two girls, and they sat looking for lice on each other's heads. The boy was frightened by seeing still more people coming out of the tusk. Some of them made rice, some fixed meat, some cut firewood, and some got water.

Seeing all this, the younger boy slipped out and ran to his older brother. "Oh, brother," he cried. "A lot of people just came out of the tusk!"

"Why didn't you grab them?" asked his brother.

"I was too afraid; I didn't dare," he replied.

So the older boy said, "Let me go hide and see about this." A little later, when the brother was hiding, he saw a girl come out of the tusk. He reached out and grabbed her. "We'll get married," he declared.

But the girl exclaimed, "No! We can't possibly."

Finally, however, he prevailed, and they were married. All of the people from inside the tusk came out to help celebrate. They ate the wedding feast and stayed for two or three more days.

One day the boys' father and Dararint sent their dog to the children. When the dog arrived, the older boy told him to go back home and tell his father and Dararint to come visit him. The dog agreed to carry the message.

So he went back to them, saying, "Your child told me to tell you to come to him."

So the father and his wife prepared to go. When they finally arrived at the boy's house, he poured wine and roasted a pig for them. However, he made a crock of bad wine and a crock of good wine. To his father the boy gave the good wine, but to Dararint he gave the bad wine. When both of them had finished eating and drinking, and were preparing to return home, the boy pleaded, "Stay a little longer, father."

But the boy could not persuade Dararint to stay. "We have to go home to take care of the pigs and chickens," she insisted.

"The water is very high," the child countered.

"Never mind the water," she said. "If it comes to my waist, I'll walk sideways. If it comes to my neck, I'll swim."

Seeing that she was determined to go, the boy measured out some rice for his father. But for Dararint he measured out sand and put it in the bottom of her basket.

On their way home, they had gone halfway across the river when suddenly they both sank in the water. And so they died.

THE MONKEY MIDWIFE

This story in Roglai was told by Mr. A. Y.,
and was translated by Maxwell Cobbey.

Our ancestors have told about the old life for the benefit of people today.

In the old days, a man would ask for a woman's hand in marriage, pay the bride-price, and then there would be a wedding feast. After the feast, they would exchange bracelets.

Later, when the wife was pregnant and about to give birth, they would call all the relatives to come and cut her open to take the child out to care for it. As for the mother, she would die and someone would bury her.

Everyone did things that way. Even though the husband and wife really loved each other, they would always be torn apart by the birth of their first child. It was very strange in those days--people were mourning the death of someone everyday.

In those days there lived a young man and his wife, who had been married only a year. The wife was now nine months pregnant and just about to give birth. So the husband sharpened his knife and went to call all of the relatives on his wife's side to come and help cut open his wife and take the child out. The husband was very sad, knowing that he would soon lose his wife.

The relatives came. And when someone cut open his wife, she died. Then they went to get some bark of a tree in order to wrap up her body and bury it. There was much weeping and wailing as they went together to bury her. They wept and wept as they went along, carrying her body on a pole between them, on their way to the bamboo clump.

There they met a group of monkeys who asked, "Why are you all wailing so terribly every day?"

"That's the way it has to be," the people answered. "When someone is pregnant, we must cut her open and take out the child."

22

"If you do that, you will never have many offspring," countered one of the female monkeys.

"That's true, ma'am."

"You all aren't thinking. Why have you been killing each other like that? It will be the end of the human race! This is what you must do. When a woman's time to give birth has come, her husband must get a new pot, pure water, and she must drink pure water only. Then when she is in labor, work to help her take the child out. The feces and urine of the child will come out. Then look for the umbilical cord, pull it far out to the knees, then cut it off. Take a vine and tie the cord off halfway."

"As for the mother, pour her hot water to drink and put pressure on her stomach. Her own mother should do this, or her husband can help. There are certain foods she should not eat: eggplant, fish sauce, aged meat, and all kinds of strong meat are forbidden."

When the monkey woman finished speaking, the people dug a grave and buried the body they had been carrying. Then the person in charge of the burial spoke to the monkey.

"Oh, ma'am, we have some among us who are pregnant and about to give birth. I don't suppose you would come and help us, would you?"

"Why not? I'll come. Only I'm afraid of the ogdays." (She said 'dogs' in a pig latin way to keep the dogs themselves from understanding what the conversation was about.)

The leader of the burial understood immediately. "Don't worry," he assured her. "When you come, we will shut up everything."

"Okay, then I can come. Whenever someone is about to give birth, you all come call me from here at this clump of bamboo. Meanwhile I'll stay right here and find fruit and bamboo sprouts to eat."

The person in charge of the burial wanted to make sure, so he asked again, "This is for sure now? When a woman is about to give birth, I'll come here and knock on the bamboo. And when you here, you'll come, right?"

"Yes, that's right," assented the monkey-woman.

So when the next woman began labor, everything took place as arranged. Arriving at the clump of bamboo, the people knocked three times on a dead bamboo. Then as she had promised, the monkey came up to them and asked, "Have you really shut everything up?"

"Yes, it's all taken care of."

So the monkey came along to the house. The master's dogs had all been tied and stowed above the rafters.

Some people entered the house and got betel nut for the monkey to chew.

Meanwhile, the woman was in pain, about at the point of delivery, and she was crying out, "Oh, oh!" So the monkey lady chewed her betel nut quickly and went to her. She urged all the people to pour hot water and to get a vine for tying the umbilical cord and a bamboo chopping block for cutting it off.

The woman's husband was very busy preparing a meal: cutting wood, fixing rice, scouring the pot and the bowls. He was so busy he would do something and then forget whether he'd done it or not.

Then the child came out. When the monkey woman saw the newborn's feces and urine coming out, she said, "Make a pouch out of cloth for me to use to take the feces and urine and bury them at the base of the house ladder."

So they got busy with a spade and dug a hole to bury the pouch. When they had finished, the monkey lady advised the mothers, "From the day a child is born until your blood is dry you must not take a bath or wash in the river. Don't eat anything strong-smelling, neither eggplant nor fish sauce or anything like that. Just eat rice with salt and drink hot water."

"When you go to bury the feces and urine of the child," she continued, "don't look to the left or right, lest it make the child squint-eyed."

Having listened to the monkey woman's advice, they took two hens and roasted them for her to eat. Then they divined by using the jaws of the chickens. And what a lucky omen it gave!

The next morning, the monkey lady was getting ready to go home when the husband came and said to her, "Seven days from now please bring all your relatives and come to eat and drink with us." The monkey lady agreed and went home.

The husband first gathered together a lot of shirts and skirts and set them aside. Then he said to himself, "Who knows whether they will eat a lot or a little? So he went and borrowed wine jars from people and had two or three jars full of wine. He brought them and put them at the posts of the house, along with a lot of pigs and chickens. But all of the dogs he tied up and put up on the rafters above the kitchen area where they remained for several days after having had one last good meal. About eight o'clock in the morning on the day of the feast, the people heard the chatter of the monkeys as they came to the feast. There were children, mothers, and fathers. The monkey midwife arrived first. The master of the house called for her to enter, and then they all came in. The master of the house proffered tobacco and betel nut. Then all the cooks got up together and roasted the pigs and chickens, urging each other all the while, "Hurry up! The guests are hungry!"

All of the monkeys chatted with the elders there. They noticed the dogs tied up in the rafters out of the way.

The master of the house was in charge of the food preparation. Soon they dished up the rice and vegetables and insisted that the monkey lady start first and that the monkey elders be next. After the meal, they presented the clothes to the monkey midwife.

Then they all assembled to drink the wine. They drank and drank, so much that they could no longer walk. "What should be done?" the people wondered. It was almost dark, so they invited the monkeys to spend the night with them, but the monkeys refused, shaking their heads. It was impossible for them to spend the night, they said. So they said good-bye, and the people gave them legs of pork and chicken to take along home.

They went out of the house, but got only about fifty yards because they were very drunk. Because they were so drunk, they couldn't see straight; not a monkey was able to make it home. About that time the master of the house released the dogs. The dogs chased and bit the monkeys, scattering all the pork and chicken.

It was most pitiful. Nearly all the monkeys died--fifty or a hundred maybe, I don't know exactly. But two little ones got away--a male and a female. Because they were just baby monkeys, they hadn't had any wine to drink and were able to scramble up a tree when the dogs came after them. All of the adult monkeys were drunk and died from dog bites. The two that got away later had many offspring, and these offspring are the monkeys we know nowadays.

In the old days, people didn't know how to take care of each other when someone was about to have a baby. They used to cut open the mother and take out the child. This is the story about the monkey midwife who took care of expectant mothers in the old days.

MASTER THUAN AND THE TIGER FAIRY

This story was told in Jeh by an old man from
Dak Trap and was translated by Patrick Cohen.

This is the legend of two brothers who went to pick mangoes long ago.

On their way to pick fruit, the brothers came to a mango tree. They climbed the tree and began to pick. Suddenly there appeared a man-eating phantom. Quickly the brothers climbed up higher in the tree and began to pitch mangoes at the phantom to frighten it away. All night long the brothers stayed up in the tree.

The next morning, the phantom returned, but then it disappeared into a hole and didn't come out again. Since they could see no sign of it, the brothers climbed down out of the tree and went home.

They summoned the other villagers: "Come on everyone! Let's go look at the man-eating phantom that just ran into a hole out there."

When the villagers arrived, they found the phantom just as the brothers had said. Then they began to cut trees and gather materials for a big fire that they intended to build over the phantom's hole to burn it up. With everything ready, the villagers said to the short-tailed shrew, "You go in and look first." So the shrew went in, but he heard something that scared him, and he ran out.

Then the two brothers ordered a squirrel to go and look. The squirrel went in, also heard something that scared him, and ran back out.

Finally, the chipmunk volunteered to go, and the brothers consented to let him try. Bravely the chipmunk entered the hole, but only a few moments later he too dashed out again.

"That chipmunk talked so bravely a minute ago," jeered the brothers, "but he really isn't so brave!"

26

So the chipmunk went back in. This time he entered cautiously. Inside, he saw a beautiful young woman. He ran back out and told the brothers what he had seen. The brothers went in to see for themselves, and sure enough, there was a beautiful young woman!

The older brother then took his younger brother, Master Thuan, and gave him to the beautiful young woman as her husband. What neither brother knew was that the young woman in reality was the tiger fairy. They all went back to the village, unaware that a tigress accompanied them.

One day the tiger fairy urged Master Thuan, "Let's go pick fruit." But young Thuan said, "Not just now." Then later he felt like going, so he said, "Let's go." And the two of them set off.

Soon they came to the same mango tree that the two brothers had previously climbed. Master Thuan climbed up into the tree while the tiger fairy remained on the ground. But while he was climbing, the fairy shook her body and turned into a tigress. Seeing what had happened, Thuan kept on climbing to try to get away from her. The tigress started up the tree in hot pursuit, intending to eat him.

"That old woman!" Thuan said dejectedly. "I didn't know before what she was really like. Now I know for sure that she can turn into a tigress in order to eat us."

So Master Thuan turned himself into a mango and called to a crow, "Oh crow. Take this mango that's really me and drop it at the edge of the river." And the crow obligingly did as he was asked.

When the tigress saw what was happening, she growled furiously and followed on the ground while the crow flew above. She followed until the crow dropped the mango at the river's edge as instructed. Then the crow flew off.

Since the tiger fairy hadn't seen just where the mango had fallen, she lingered awhile in the area. While she was waiting, one of the king's slaves came to get water. As the slave came closer and closer to the water's edge, the tiger fairy's body changed a bit more into the figure of a woman until finally he saw the tiger fairy as a beautiful woman coming up out of the water hole.

The slave hurried home and called the king, "Oh, king! Come and see the most beautiful woman you've ever seen."

"Where is she?"

"Down there at the water hole."

So the king went down to see for himself. When he arrived at the place where the slave had seen the fairy, and he saw her, he went to her and said, "Will you marry me?"

"Get your family to make a dam across the river to catch a lot of fish. Then I will marry you."

Agreeing to this condition, the king called his family together and told them to build a dam across the river that would catch a lot of fish. When the dam had been built, the fairy instructed the family to gather up all the fish that had been caught. Then she cut open each fish to see if it had eaten the mango which was Master Thuan. She inspected all of the fish's intestines, but the mango was not there.

Soon afterward the tiger fairy married the king and went to live in his village. She refused to enter his house, however, but stayed down by the village fence.

Once she changed herself into a tigress and asked two children coming home from gathering vegetables, "When you were out, did you happen to find a mango that someone had thrown away?"

"No," the children replied. "We haven't seen a mango like that."

Not trusting them, the tiger asked to look at the things in their bamboo container. The children turned the container upside down and spilled the contents on the ground for her to see. But the tiger fairy saw only vegetables.

"Oh you two! You really did find the mango. Why are you lying to me?"

"Of course we haven't seen it!" the children insisted. "If we had seen it, we would have told you."

Now as a matter of fact, the children had really found the mango and had hidden it under some vegetable leaves. When the tiger fairy looked everything over, she had missed it. After their encounter with the tiger fairy, the children went on home to their grandmother.

Emptying out their things, they called, "Oh grandmother! Look at what we've found!"

"Shh! Don't talk about it. The tiger fairy might hear," cautioned the grandmother.

But the tiger fairy had already overheard and came up to the grandchildren. "What were you talking about?" she asked.

"Oh, nothing. We were just fooling around."

But the tiger fairy replied, "I heard your grandmother talking with you just now.

So the grandmother said, "My grandchildren were just talking nonsense, like kids do, you know."

But the grandmother had already taken precautions. When she heard her grandchildren talking to the tigress, she had taken the mango and put it into a wine jar, then clapped the lid over the mouth of the jar. The tiger fairy looked around and listened, but, not finding anything, she went home.

When she had gone, the grandchildren took the mango from the wine jar and cut it open to look at it. And there was Master Thuan! They put the mango back into the wine jar and waited.

The next day the grandchildren peeked into the jar, and the day after that they peeked at it again. On the third day when they looked again, the mango popped open and turned itself into Master Thuan again.

The next day Master Thuan was up and washing his face near the door of the house when the tiger fairy caught sight of him. "Oh, Master Thuan!" she called. "Where have you been? You weren't inside the house before, and every day I've been looking for you."

"Oh, I was right here all the time."

Now the fairy asked him to tell her where he slept, on the pretext that she would bring him his tobacco. Master Thuan told her that he slept in the communal house. That night she went to the communal house pretending to bring tobacco to Master Thuan, but of course that wasn't her real reason. The tigress pounced on the sleeping form of one of the king's slaves and proceeded to eat him up, thinking she was eating Master Thuan.

"Now I've finally eaten you up, Master Thuan," she gloated.

Young Thuan had heard all the commotion and knew that the tiger fairy had come to eat him, but had made a mistake. Gloomily he thought, "One of these days she's going to get me."

The next day Master Thuan was again washing his face by the door when the tiger fairy, who was down by the fence, saw him. She came up to him, "Where did you sleep last night? I came to bring you tobacco but couldn't find you."

Master Thuan replied that, as always, he had slept in the communal house.

Then the tiger fairy ordered Master Thuan to carry a letter to her village. So he took his machete and sharpened it well. Then he started off for the village where the tiger fairy's people lived. He travelled on and on until, exhausted, he lay down and slept on a large rock. As he slept, he dreamed. In his dreams, a spirit came to him and warned, "You must not go into the tiger village or one of them might eat you up. They will want to eat you because of the contents of the letter you are carrying." The spirit then wrote another letter and gave it to Master Thuan in place of the original.

The next morning, Master Thuan took the letter and resumed his journey. Eventually he arrived at the tiger fairy's village. The tigers all came out to meet him, wanting to eat him up.

But the village leaders wouldn't have it. "No, not yet. Let's have a look at the letter first." So the leaders took the letter from Master Thuan and read it. "He's not the right one to eat," they told the others.

The young tigers stood around, drooling at the mouth and saying, "Let's eat him anyway." But the leaders wouldn't allow it.

Later that night Master Thuan was sleeping in the communal house when he noticed a lot of baskets hanging from the rafters. "What are those baskets hanging there for?" he inquired.

"Oh, those are the baskets that we strike to make things," they replied. "Our whole village produces tigers like that. And these baskets can also turn into mountains." Then they all went to sleep.

At dawn Master Thuan got up and struck all the baskets, making mountains and hills all around. Now the village wouldn't be able to make tigers the way they had previously. After that powerful act, Master Thuan fled the village of the tigers and returned home.

When he arrived home, the tiger fairy asked him, "Did you deliver the letter or not?"

"Oh, yes," answered Master Thuan. "I gave it to them." His response made the tiger fairy puzzled as to why they hadn't eaten him up.

The next day the tiger fairy pretended to be sick. She just lay there and moaned a lot. Then she ordered the king to call Master Thuan. No sooner had she made her demand, than the king was on his way to carry out her wish.

"Oh Master Thuan," called the king. "The queen sent me to call for you."

"What does she want?" asked Master Thuan.

"The queen says she is very sick," replied the king.

So Master Thuan went down to see if she was really sick or just pretending.

Sometime later the tiger fairy groaned, "Oh, I am dying. Go and call Master Thuan."

So once again the king went out and called, "Oh, Master Thuan, the queen has died at last. She urged me before she died to tell you to come."

Master Thuan and his friends, however, just continued sharpening their machetes on a whetstone as they smoked their pipes. Then when they had finished smoking, they got up and went to see the tiger fairy. Sure enough, she appeared to be dead! So they tied her legs together and carried her out on a pole to bury her.

But on the way to the graveyard, the tiger fairy came to life and broke the ropes tied around her. Then she changed into a ferocious tiger anxious to eat them up. Then she changed her mind and decided to return to her own people, the tigers.

But the two brothers quickly drew out their sharpened machetes and began hacking up the tiger fairy. One piece became two, two pieces became three, three became four, and finally there were many, many pieces. They had killed the tiger fairy once and for all.

The king's slaves had followed the two brothers and now reported to him, "Oh king, look! The two brothers have just hacked your wife to pieces down there!"

"Why did they do that?" demanded the king angrily.

"Because she turned into a tiger," they replied.

When the two brothers returned, the king shouted to them, "Why did you chop up my wife?"

"Why don't you go and count your slaves?" the brothers retorted.

When the king counted his slaves, he discovered that two were missing. The brothers told him that the tiger fairy had eaten them.

Thus the king, who had acted so foolishly, lost out. He was now very poor so he could no longer be king. Then all of the villagers had a big celebration with lots of drinking and eating and partying in anticipation of a new king.

THE CORD THAT TIES PEOPLE TOGETHER

This story was told in Mnong Rlam by a high school
student, and was translated by Evangeline Blood.

There once was an old man who lived in a large tree in the
spirit village. He always carried a lot of cords in his hand, and
people said that he used these cords to tie the souls of a boy and
a girl together while they were still young. For this purpose, the
old man kept a book in which all the names of newly born children
were recorded.

One day a young boy followed his older brother up the mountain,
but he wasn't able to keep up. When he knew he was lost, he sought
shelter in a cave, and inside the cave he saw the spirit village.
Then the spirits came and took him and washed his face. Soon
nearly all of them left for work, but a few of them stayed at the
houses.

The boy saw an old man sitting in the shadow of a large tree in
the middle of the village, so he went up to him and asked,
"Grandfather Mbieng, why are you here?"

"I am here to tie promised children together for marriage," the
old man replied. "I tie the girl's finger to the thumb of the boy.
Later when they are old enough, they marry."

"Have you tied me yet?" the boy asked.

"What is your name?" inquired Grandfather Mbieng.

"My name is Dong, the child of Ing. I live in Boc village."

Grandfather Mbieng took his book, opened it, and read the boy's
name. Then he said, "I have promised you to Dan, the child of a
poor person. She is fatherless and she lives in Mham village. I
have fastened you with a white cord so that later on the two of
you will live well and be rich. When I tie people with red or
black cords, they die early and never have much; only a white cord
is able to give good things."

32

"Oh, thank you, Grandfather. Now please let me return to my village. Please be so kind as to show me the road and guide me home."

"Go to the gateway of this village," instructed the old man, "then close your eyes and open them, and you will be right at the gate of your house."

So the boy left and did just what the old man had told him to do. He went outside the gate of the spirit village, shut his eyes, and waited five minutes. Then he opened his eyes and saw that he was in his own village, just as the old man had promised.

When he told his brother and the other villagers what he had seen, they, too, wanted to find out about the wives intended for them. So they went to the old man and asked him many questions. But later they were all too shy to talk about which girls he had tied them to.

Being curious to see what his wife-to-be looked like, Dong went to Dan's village and stayed there three days. Finally, he saw her. She had white skin, but she was still just a child and didn't know how to take care of herself very well. Her face was dirty and she lacked proper food and clothing. Moreover, she had no father: she was the illegitimate child of a loose woman.

Dong watched as she went down to the river to bathe. When she got to the edge of the water, he ran up behind her and hit her with a stick. She fell down dead and was swept away by the current. Dong threw her clothes in after her and went home. Nobody had seen him hit her, and no one in Mham village ever saw Dan again.

The water swept Dan to the village of U. Two girls were getting water when they spotted her body. They took her out of the water and carried her up onto the bank. Then she started to breathe again and speak. The girls were delighted! Since Dan was still just a child, not quite seven years old, the girls took her to the king. And because the king had no children, he adopted her as his own and renamed her Bia-Klui.

There she grew up into a very pretty young lady, and all of the boys liked her, but she had no wish to marry. After some time the king died, leaving only Bia-Klui to succeed him. But the general and others who had worked for the king wanted to take over themselves. They made plans to assassinate the would-be queen, but she managed to escape and went to hide in the forest.

There she met a very handsome young man, the son of the king of Boc village. "What are you doing here?" he asked.

Briefly, she told him her story. "I am the child of the king of U village. When my father died, the officers and the palace attendants took over. They planned to kill me to keep me from

becoming queen. I knew about their plan, so I got away secretly to
this place, hoping to find someone who could help me."

Upon hearing this, the young man took her with him on his horse
and rode back to his village. He arranged for her to stay at his
parents' house, then asked his father for some soldiers.

Together with the soldiers he went to fight the usurpers of U
village. The battle lasted three days, until the soldiers had
destroyed the whole village with their swords and spears. All of
the officers and former councilors of the king were killed. After
his great victory, the young prince, who was really Dong, called
for the king's child, and the people welcomed Bia-Klui back to U.

Then Bia-Klui married Dong and made him king. As king, Dong
repaired the village and made it very beautiful. But soon after,
because Bia-Klui was so very beautiful, Dong forgot all about his
public works. All he thought about and worked for was his wife. He
held a lot of big feasts and collected a lot of taxes. This made
the villagers angry with him, and they wanted to overthrow him,
but they couldn't. When they refused to pay their taxes, King Dong
came himself with soldiers and fought with them. After that, there
was peace.

When they had been married some time, Bia-Klui had a beautiful
baby boy, whom they named Yang. When he grew up, he was very
skillful and went off to distant place to fight.

One day Bia-Klui told her husband the story of her life.
"Brother Dong, would you like to hear about my life from girlhood
until I met you?" she asked.

"Yes, I would like to very much," he answered.

"Years ago, when I was a small child I lived with my mother in
Mham village. I didn't have a father. When I was seven years old,
a boy hit me on the back and I died. He wasn't very big--maybe
only eight or nine years old--and I didn't know he was behind me.
I didn't recognize him because he was from a distant village.

"Then I was swept away by the water to U village where two
girls found me as they were getting water. These girls lived with
the king, and as he had no children, he adopted me. I grew up to
be very beautiful and had many suitors, but I didn't want any of
them. Then the day came when my father the king died. I should
have succeeded him, but my officers and councilors rebelled
because they did not want a woman ruling over men. They wanted to
kill me, so I left the house secretly without anyone seeing me. I
stayed three days in the woods then I met you. So you can see that
I have had a hard life."

As Dong was listening to his wife's account, his mind was
thinking of many things. One thing he was sure of was that the old
man's words had come true.

"What is your real name?" he asked.

"My name is Dan."

Dong knew that she was perfectly correct. Then he told her all about his own life, all that he had seen and done.

And from that day on everyone knew that tied-cord engagements were valid.

THE GOLD MINE

This story, told in Nung by a forty-year-old
man, was translated by Janice Saul.

Once upon a time there were two brothers whose mother and father had died. The older brother was greedy and took all of the parents' possessions; he didn't give his younger brother anything except an axe. Each day the younger brother took the axe and went to cut firewood to sell, so he would have food to eat.

One day when he went out to cut firewood as usual, he saw a peach tree laden with very ripe fruit. He climbed the tree, picked some of the fruit, and ate it. Then he fell asleep in the tree.

Soon a group of monkeys came along to pick some of the fruit. When they saw the boy sleeping soundly, they said to each other, "This person is dead already. Shall we take him to a silver mine or a gold mine to bury him?"

One monkey suggested the gold mine. So they carried the boy off to a gold mine and buried him there. When the boy awoke, he saw that he was surrounded by gold. Since there was so much gold all around, he picked some of it up and took it home.

When the day arrived for the anniversary celebration of his father's death, the younger brother cooked a special memorial feast and invited his older brother to come and eat with him.

But the older brother said, "You are a poor man without anything. How is it that you are able to afford this memorial feast and invite me to come and eat with you? However, if you will bring some gold and fasten it to the doorway then I will come to eat."

So the younger brother did as the older brother requested. And when the older brother went to the feast, he saw that there was a great deal of gold. Now he became very envious.

"Where did you did this gold?" he asked.

"One day I went out to cut firewood," replied the younger brother, "and I saw a peach tree full of ripe fruit. So I climbed

36

the tree, ate some peaches, and then fell sound asleep in the top
of the tree. Then along came a group of monkeys and carried me to
a gold mine and left me there. When I awoke, I took some of the
gold and brought it home."

The older brother decided to try the same thing. So one day he
went to the peach tree and ate some of the fruit. Then he slept as
his younger brother had done. Again the monkeys arrived and saw
him there sleeping. When they had finished eating, they asked each
other, "To which mine shall we carry him?"

One monkey said, "To the silver mine."

Then the older brother cried out, "Carry me to the gold mine!"

"He's not dead at all--he's still alive!" the monkeys exclaimed.

So they pushed the elder brother out of the tree, and he fell
to his death.

THE STORY OF PHUONG LOIH

This story was told in Haroi by a young married
man and was translated by Hella Goschnick.

One day Phuong Loih went to weed a field with his grandmother. When some black ants bit her, Phuong Loih became very angry.

"How dare these black ants bite my grandmother! I'll show them! I'll take them and sell them right away."

So he gathered up the black ants and went to a village. When people there inquired, "Who is there?" he answered, "It's me."

"Come in and stay awhile," they said. So he went in.

"Where shall I leave my ants?" he asked.

"Just put them over there in the corner."

So he did as they told him, but a chicken ate up all of the ants.

"Hey," said Phuong Loih, "your chicken ate my ants."

"If the chicken ate your ants, then of course you must take the chicken in return," the villagers replied.

So Phuong Loih took the chicken and went to sell it at another village. "Where are you going?" the people there asked him.

"I'm going to sell a chicken," he replied. So they invited him in, and he accepted their invitation.

Then he asked them where he could put his chicken. When they told him to put it in the corner, Phuong Loih did so, but a dog bit the chicken and it died. So he complained, and the people offered him the dog as payment. Phuong Loih took the dog and went on to another village, intending to sell it there.

Again he was invited in, and he asked where he could put the dog.

"Leave it outside," they said, so he did. But the dog was

38

bitten by a pig. When Phuong Loih complained, they let him have the pig that had done the damage.

Then he left to sell the pig in another village. When he was invited to come in, he asked where he could leave his pig, and they told him to leave it away from the house. He did so, but a goat butted it and killed it. So the people in that village gave him the goat.

On went Phuong Loih to another place to sell the goat. Again he asked where he could leave his animal, and they replied, "Just leave it outside there." So he did, but then a bull gored it. Of course, then, the villagers gave him the bull.

When he arrived at a different village to sell the bull, again he was invited in. They told him to tie his bull in the meadow. There a horse kicked it to death, so Phuong Loih was given the horse in return.

He went on his way to sell the horse at still another village. There he was received, and the villagers told him to tie his horse in the meadow. But a water buffalo killed it by goring it to death, so the villagers gave him the buffalo.

On to the next village he went to sell the buffalo. There he was told to tie the water buffalo in the forest a little ways off. An elephant trampled the buffalo to death, so they gave Phuong Loih the elephant instead.

Then he went to the next village to sell the elephant. When he asked where he should leave it, they told him to tie it at the edge of the village. He did, but then they started to play gongs in the village, and that scared the elephant so that it ran away. So the villagers had to give him the gongs.

He carried the gongs on his back to the next village to sell them. There they told him to put the gongs down in the corner of the house, but someone dropped the mortar on the gongs and they were ruined. So Phuong Loih was given the mortar as compensation.

He carried the mortar on to the next village, where he was told to put it down in the corner of a house. Then sparks from the fire burned the mortar. So the villagers gave him the embers in return.

Then Phuong Loih left to sell his fire in the next village. The people there asked him in and told him to put his embers in the corner of the house. There someone spilled water which put out the fire, so they gave Phuong Loih a mouthful of water to take in return.

On his way to sell the water he met five young girls. They started to laugh and Phuong Loih laughed with them and so spilled the water. When he blamed them for making him lose his water, they said, "Take all five of us."

So he put all five girls into the basket on his back and went on. Soon they came to a mango tree. The girls asked him to stop so they could pick some mangoes. He stopped and the girls climbed the tree. When they dropped mangoes into the basket on his back, Phuong Loih thought it was the girls jumping back into the basket. So he went on without them.

Then he carried the mangoes back to his grandmother. He told her to spread her legs to receive the girls in her lap. But she replied, "What are you talking about--five young girls? You've only got mangoes in your basket."

Then Phuong Loih untied the basket from his back, threw it down full of mangoes on his grandmother's lap, and killed her.

THE MONKEY GIRL

This story was told in Tho by H:v.C.
and was translated by Colin Day.

Once upon a time there was a king whose name was Than Nhac. He had three sons: Lord One, who was the eldest, and his brothers Lord Two and Lord Three. The two older brothers were married, but Lord Three had no wife, though he was the most handsome young man in all the world. The longer one looked at him, the handsomer he seemed.

But not only was Lord Three not married, he had no interest in girls. He cared only for his work.

Then one day Lord Three went to the market. There he met a very old woman selling bamboo mats, and he asked her, "Where do you get those mats to sell, Granny?"

"In the forest where I live," she replied, "there is a girl monkey who weaves them for me to sell. I do not make them myself."

"When you go home, please ask her if she could possibly weave a mat to fit my bed exactly. Then when you return, please let me know."

The next morning the old woman returned with the mat. The girl monkey had woven it immediately. When Lord Three tried it, it fit exactly. The bed was square, and all four corners of the mat fit perfectly at the first try. It was neither too large nor too small.

"Granny, Granny," he asked excitedly, "do you know where this girl lives?"

"It is very far away," the old woman replied. "She lives in a big forest by herself. Since she can't sell the mats herself, she weaves them and gives them to me to sell. But she's not really a person, you know, only a monkey."

"Direct me to where she lives, Granny."

"She lives by herself in the old part of the forest."

Then Lord Three called out the army to surround the forest. He went in alone to search. He found no people there, only a girl monkey. She was a pretty monkey, but a monkey just the same. Lord Three arrested her and was about to tie her up when she spoke up, "Young man, if you had such a desire to find me, you need not tie me up. You need only tell me to come with you."

"All right, if you say so," he replied. And they walked out of the forest.

"Now we'll walk back to the palace," declared Lord Three.

"There is no need for this army," she replied. "If you want me to go with you, first send this army back home. Then we will go back together."

So Lord Three summoned all the army and commanded them to return to their barracks. So just the two of them were left. Then the girl monkey said, "Close your eyes, and we will wait for the wind."

No sooner had they shut their eyes than a great gust of wind came up and blew them instantly to the palace. It was a magic wind that took them to Lord Three's home.

A little later Lord One and Lord Two were having a discussion with their father the king.

"It will not do," said the king. "We must think of a ruse to get him to take a wife. Lord Three would not marry anyone, however beautiful, and now why does he want to marry a monkey? We must force him to take a real wife. We'll have a wife contest! That will do it. It will never do for him not to marry."

The king announced to his three sons that the wife contest was to see which of them had the most beautiful wife. He set the date for three months hence. At that time each of his sons was to have a wife ready to bring to the palace, and the generals would judge which one was the most beautiful.

But Lord Three said, "Please, let us have the contest as early as possible. Let's have it tomorrow and not wait such a long time."

"But," the king protested, "you do not yet have a wife. Why should we have the contest tomorrow?"

"Whether I have a wife yet is not important. Please, let's have the contest tomorrow. Let's not wait such a long time."

"Oh, all right then," the king consented, "tomorrow we will have the contest. Tomorrow morning at eight o'clock we'll begin. Lord One, Lord Two, and Lord Three, have your wives here at eight o'clock for the judging."

So Lord One and Lord Two got their wives ready for the contest. When their dresses and finery were arranged just right, they went to appear before the judges. The eldest son took his wife in first before all of the officials who were in their places all around the room. The king was there too, seated with the generals on one side. Lord One's wife was not pretty. She had a mouth which was slightly twisted.

Then Lord Two brought in his wife to be judged, but she had a high forehead and was not beautiful. The judges did not think either of these wives could receive first place.

Then the king and the generals remarked, "Why is it that Lord One and Lord Two are here, but Lord Three has not yet arrived?"

They sent some soldiers to his house to fetch him. "It is time, you know. The contest is in progress. Why have you not yet come? Why are you still here at home?"

"I know they are having the contest," replied Lord Three, "but I must have a hammock to carry my wife there. She can't walk."

So four soldiers carried Lord Three's wife from the house. Before, she had appeared to be a monkey, but she was really a fairy who had turned into a monkey. Now when they brought her before all of the generals, the king could not bear to look at her for her beauty. All of the judges saw that Lord Three's wife was the most beautiful of all. Indeed, there was no one in the whole world quite so beautiful because she was a fairy, and the beauty of fairies surpasses that of mere mortals. So Lord Three's wife won first place in the contest.

Then Lord Three went back immediately to get her monkey skin, and he chopped it into shreds.

PO-ONG'S STOLEN RICE HOUSE or
THE TRIUMPH OF THE FAMISHED OVER THE RICH

This story was told in Sedang by the now-deceased
Hmou when he was twenty-five years old. It was
translated by Kenneth Smith.

Once upon a time there were two brothers, Teang and his younger brother, Sie.

One year there was a terrible famine. No one had any rice to eat and everyone was hungry. Since there was no other kind of work to do, the people worked in the communal house making all kinds of baskets and trays. The rest of the time they just slept because there wasn't anything to eat.

Both Teang and Sie were married and lived in the same house with their wives. One day Sie said to his older brother, "Teang, you stay and guard the house while I go with my wife to look for wild potatoes, okay? We want to find some potatoes to eat today."

"All right," Teang agreed, and Sie left with his wife. After a while they returned home and cooked everything they had found that day. When the food was ready, Sie's wife called Teang.

"Brother-in-law, come in and eat potatoes and other things with us."

But when Teang went to eat, there were no potatoes, only rice. Every day it was the same. Sie's wife would call him to eat potatoes, but instead she served rice.

So one day Teang said, "Tell me what you two are up to. Every day you say that you're going to look for potatoes. But I never see any of these potatoes and we only eat rice. How is it that you have rice when no one has any this year? Where are you getting it, when everyone around here is starving?"

So Sie told his brother the truth. "We are getting some of Po-ong's rice up there. Each day we go up and get just one basketful."

44

"Where is his rice house?" queried Teang.

"Up there," answered Sie.

"Well, tomorrow show me, okay? I want to go up and get a lot."

So the next day Sie went up there with Teang.

"Here's the rice house," said Sie. "See how very large it is! I can't imagine how many baskets of rice must be in it--certainly five hundred or eight hundred medium-sized basketfuls."

At first, Teang wanted to carry out just one medium-sized basket, but then that didn't seem enough to him. So he thought he'd take two. But that didn't seem enough either. Finally, he decided that he'd have to carry out one very large basket.

But even as he made the decision, he said, "Surely this still is not enough. Nevertheless, sister-in-law, peel off a piece of the string-bark down there. I want to carry one very large back basket."

So his sister-in-law peeled off the bark as he asked. But once again Teang changed his mind.

"No, this won't do. It isn't enough. Why, we can eat one very large back basketful of rice in no time. Let's see. How much would be enough? I know. I'll carry the whole houseful of rice all at once."

We all know about Teang--how very big and strong he is. He carried that whole rice house off and set it down next to his house.

"Now we'll be able to live," he said. "No more starving. This is really living. With this, we already have enough rice for next year."

Sometime later, Po-ong wanted to sacrifice a buffalo in order to appease the spirits. He wanted to brew wine and eat buffalo, so he needed some of his rice.

"Go down and get some rice from my rice house down there," Po-ong ordered his servants and children.

A number of people went down to get the rice. All they saw were the holes where they had planted the posts for the rice house. The house had disappeared.

"Hey!" they cried. "Where has this rice house of ours gone to?"

Then they saw Teang's footprints leading away from the site. They all went home and reported, "Our rice house isn't there anymore."

Quite a few people didn't believe them. "How can anyone believe that someone carried off an entire rice house?" they scoffed. "One person? Maybe one person could carry a very large back basket of rice. He'd have to make an effort to carry even one. But a whole rice house? Impossible!"

But the others kept insisting that one person had carried off the whole rice house.

Po-ong really didn't know who to believe at first. But a man named Pokap came and told him, "I know that it was Teang who came down and stole your rice."

"Go down, Pokap," Po-ong told him, "and ask to see Teang. Ask him if it's true that he stole our rice."

Pokap then went down and called, "Teang!"

"What do you want?" replied Teang.

"Is it true that you stole our rice?"

"That's right."

"Why did you steal it?" asked Pokap.

"Why? Are you crazy? You have all sorts of things to eat. You have plenty of rice. We have nothing, no rice to keep us alive. That's why I stole your rice."

Pokap went back home because he didn't know what to answer Teang. Teang had told him the truth, and Pokap had no rebuttal. When he arrived, Po-ong asked him, "Well, is it true?"

"Yes, Teang stole the rice," replied Pokap.

So then Po-ong told Pokap to command Teang to give him loin-cloths and chickens for the rice he had stolen. Po-ong also asked for other things to compensate his loss--hoes, axes, and other tools. In fact, he told Teang to give him everything--Laotian-style blankets included--in addition to returning the rice.

"Tell him that if he doesn't want to return the rice, then we'll kill him," Po-ong said.

Pokap went down once again and delivered Po-ong's ultimatum.

"Po-ong demands that you give him ten hoes, ten axes, ten chickens, ten of everything. And if you don't, we'll come down here and fight you."

"He talks like that, does he? Well, let me tell you something. I'll give you one baby chick that was just hatched yesterday, and that's it. I'll not give him one thing more for the rice I stole."

"No," replied Pokap, "that won't do." So Pokap went back and reported to Po-ong.

"He has belittled and ridiculed us," said Pokap, "so now we must fight them."

"If you want to fight, then fight," answered Po-ong.

Once again Pokap went down to talk with Teang.

"Po-ong refuses your offer. If you still aren't willing to return his rice and make compensation, he'll have to fight you."

"If you want to fight me, why not? It doesn't matter to me. Why should I care when I'm dying of hunger."

One night when Teang was sleep in the communal house, Po-ong's men went down and encircled the building. They were all over--at his gate, everywhere!

"Oh, Teang," they called, "get up, get up! We want to fight now."

When Teang looked out and saw the hordes of people, he went quickly and got his sword. It was a huge sword--like the leaf of a banana plant--just enormous! But instead of using his sword he lifted his crossbow and shot into a branch of a large tree, severing it. The branch fell on Po-ong's men and killed a great many of them. When the rest of them saw this, they fled.

They went back and told Po-ong, "We can't fight Teang! He's amazing! With just one arrow of his crossbow he killed many of us. We can't possibly win in a fight against a man like that!"

"Hmmm," said Po-ong, "if that's the way it is, I'll make friends with him. We'll become just like father and son. Pokap, go down and ask Teang if he wants to become like my son. Explain that because many of my servants are now dead, I want us to be like father and son."

Pokap delivered the message, but Teang didn't believe him.

"You're lying," he accused him. "Really, you want to kill me."

"No," Pokap replied, "he won't kill you. He wants very much for you two to be like father and son. If he fights someone in the future, he wants you on his side. You're big and strong."

"Well, if that's the way it really is, then okay. Tell Po-ong that I would like to have a father-son relationship with him."

"He agrees!" Pokap told Po-ong.

"Brew the wine!" cried Po-ong.

They brewed one hundred jugs of wine for the feast that would make Po-ong and Teang "like father and son." And while the wine was still brewing, they dug a cave in a mountainside. Later they would need this cave as a place to drink wine, because they wouldn't drink in the house.

When the wine was done, they got ready to kill the pig. "Then we must take the pig and the wine into the cave," everyone said.

"There's to be no drinking in the house, only outside in the cave."

When time for the feast came, they served up the pig and drank wine with their pork. Sie and his wife were also guests at the feast, but they weren't fooled by this show of friendliness. They knew that Po-ong and his men really wanted to kill them. They knew that he was lying when he claimed that he wanted the relationship between Teang and himself to be "like father and son." Really Po-ong was intending to kill them later. Knowing all this, Sie and his wife remained alert and only pretended to drink. They held the straw in their mouths, but they didn't swallow any wine.

Teang, on the other hand, was unaware of all this, and he drank a great deal. He drank all one hundred jugs dry. He was so drunk that he acted like a ghost.

Suddenly, some of Po-ong's men grabbed Sie and his wife and carried them into the house. But they left Teang in the cave. All of the women who had brass bracelets took them off and used them to bind Teang up. Then they took the dregs out of the hundred jars of wine and piled it on top of him. Teang was oblivious to all of this: he didn't hear a thing.

When they had dealt thus with Teang, everyone left the cave, closing up the entrance by putting a large stone in front. Leaving Teang sealed inside, they went home.

Meanwhile, after a bit, Po-ong's men tied up Sie and his wife and put them in the communal house. Then everyone beat the drums, pounded the cymbals and gongs, and danced and danced. They were getting ready to eat Sie and his wife.

"Why did someone tell Teang to steal our rice?" someone shouted. "Why did you kill our people?"

"You have our rice and many of our things," accused another. "Now we're going to eat you tomorrow."

Talk like this went on while the drums continued to beat and the cymbals and gongs continued to be pounded. Drih, drih, drih, drih ... the sounds went on all night.

About midnight, Teang woke up because of the cold of the wine dregs that the people had poured on him. He stretched himself, and the brass wire that had bound him snapped easily.

"Isn't this something!" he exclaimed. "First he said that he wanted a relationship like father and son between us, and I thought he spoke the truth. But now I see they intend to kill me! I should never have believed them--it was all a bunch of lies!"

Teang got up in the darkness, went over, and kicked the stone away from the opening. The stone rolled down the hill, knocking

down clumps of bamboo and going on down with a koruh, koruh, koruh
sound (like the sound of gunshots).

Back in the communal house, everyone was applauding the death
of Teang. "Hurrah! Hurrah! Teang is dead!" they shouted over and
over.

Teang, of course, was not only not dead, he was at that very
moment coming toward them. On his way, Teang cut down two or three
long sections of rattan vine and carried it along with him. He
arrived at the communal house and stood there, blocking the doorway. Hearing the drih, drih of the instruments and seeing
his younger brother and wife about to be eaten, Teang called out,
"What's all this about, Po-ong? You said that you wanted us to be
friends. Now you want to kill me. At last we understand each
other."

Teang entered the house and continued, "Whoever wants to be my
slave, stand over here, and whoever doesn't want to be my slave,
stand over there."

So everyone separated themselves as he commanded. Then Teang
said to those who had indicated that they wanted to be his slaves,
"Okay, brothers. All of you take everything--the cows, the
buffalo, the chickens, the goats--everything here, and carry it
away. After you have taken everything of Po-ong's, leave and go
out on the trail."

Then Teang turned to deal with those who didn't want to be his
slaves. He took the rattan and threaded it through them like we
thread frogs. Then he led them away down paths full of stickers
and thorns. Finally, they arrived at his gate. Teang got out the
small end of the rattan and tied it up on one side of the gate.
Then he tied them up on the other side. He left them strung up
there like frogs. Teang left them there to rot, to get smelly, and
eventually to harden.

After all this, Teang was a happy man at last. He had many
buffalos and much corn. Everything that the rich Po-ong had had
now belonged to Teang. Po-ong had owned many rice houses filled
with rice. Teang now owned everything.

If Po-ong had only told the truth when he said that he wanted
to be friends with Teang, he would now be happy, too. But since he
lied and tried to kill Teang, he own "bait" destroyed him and he
lost everything he owned.

That's the end.

THE STORY OF TENG

This story was told in Brũ by various story-
tellers and was translated by Carolyn Miller.

Once an old lady and her grandson, Teng, were planting beans.
But along came a barking deer and ate up all the beans. So the old
lady and Teng set a rope trap for the barking deer and caught it.
The grandson called, "Grandmother, Grandmother, bring an axe to
cut off the head of the barking deer!" (This he said using
metaphorical language so the deer would not understand.) The deer
asked Teng, "What are you saying, friend?" To which the boy
replied, "Oh nothing, really. I'm just asking my grandmother to
bring some firewood so that we can cook some beans." The grandmother then came running with the axe poised. With one whack she
cut off the barking deer's head. The boy asked for various parts
of the deer so that he could eat them, but the grandmother
refused, giving one excuse after another. Finally, when he asked
for the intestines, the grandmother gave him permission to have
them.

As the boy was slitting and cleaning the intestines of the
barking deer, some monkeys came and asked him, "What are you
slitting, grandson of the old woman?" Teng answered politely, "Oh
nothing, really. I'm just preparing some animal intestines." They
and some other assembled animals asked him three or four times
what he was doing, and each time he answered politely. But after
they had asked him this same question several more times, the boy
became annoyed and answered crossly, "I'm slitting monkey
intestines. I'm dumping out chimpanzee intestines. I'm eating deer
liver. I'm eating barking deer liver!" At this the animals became
very angry and grabbed him crying, "Put a yoke on him! Put a yoke
on him!" So they went to cut down some heavy logs to tie around
his neck. But the boy said to them, "Don't use just any kind of
wood. In my grandmother's garden there is a Casim tree (a tree
which has very hard, heavy, red wood). Go cut some of that."

So the monkeys went and cut what they thought was the Casim
wood, but which was in reality a species of sugar cane which grows

50

very thick and big, resembling Casim wood in some superficial ways. The monkeys then tied the yoke on the boy and took him back to their village and the house of their leader.

That night while everyone was sleeping, Teng (whose yoke was not as heavy as the monkeys thought) got up and mixed sand in with the rice of the monkey's leader. In the morning, the monkeys asked Teng, "What did you dream about last night, slave lackey?" He answered, "Oh, nothing, really. I just dreamed that there was sand mixed in with the rice." The monkeys looked, and sure enough it was so.

The next night Teng quietly got up and made holes in all the cooking pots. And when the monkeys asked him the next morning, "What did you dream last night, slave lackey?" he answered, "Oh, nothing, really. I just dreamed that all the cooking pots had holes in them." The monkeys looked, and sure enough, the cooking pots all had holes.

The third night Teng put the leader's purse in the fire and burned it up. In the morning, when his captors asked him what he had dreamed the night before, Teng replied, "Oh, nothing, really. I just dreamed that the leader's purse got burned up." When the monkeys looked and found that the purse had indeed been burned, they were frightened and perplexed. They said, "How powerful this boy's dreams are!"

The next night the boy chewed on his sugar cane collar and sucked all the juice out, reducing it to a pulpy mess. When the monkeys asked him the next morning, "What did you dream last night, slave?" he replied, "I dreamed the termites ate out the yoke you put on me." The monkeys looked closely, but this time they realized what had happened and suspected that they had been tricked all along. Angrily they shouted, "Put another yoke on him and leave him for a long, long time."

When Teng heard them say this, he ran away and climbed up a big fruit tree. The monkeys, following him, called up to him, "Oh Teng! Eat the ripe fruit and throw down the green fruit." Teng threw down only one fruit and the monkeys scrambled to get it. But there were many monkeys, filling all the low bushes around. So they called up again, "Oh Teng! Eat the ripe ones but throw down the green ones." Again the monkeys scrambled to get the fruit, and again they were dissatisfied because there was not enough. Teng was afraid they would climb the tree and get not only the fruit but him also. So he called out, "Why don't you scrape the bark off the tree and urinate on the trunk so that you can climb up it?" The monkeys followed his advice only to find that they had made the trunk so slippery that they couldn't climb it.

At this point Teng called down, "Why don't you go home and get your axes and cut the tree down?" This seemed like a good idea to

them. So they all went to get their axes, leaving only one old
grandfather monkey to guard the tree and Teng. When the others had
gone, Teng slid quickly down the tree, stepping so hard on the old
grandfather monkey that it caused him to defecate. Then Teng ran
away.

When the other monkeys returned, they asked, "Where's Teng?"
The grandfather monkey, not wanting to admit what really happened,
answered, "Teng ran away. But listen! I struggled with him and
stepped on him so hard it caused him to defecate. You check and
see if I'm not telling the truth. Smell the feces. If it is foul
smelling, it is Teng's feces, but if it smells like animal fat,
it's mine." The others came up, smelled the feces, and since it
was foul-smelling (but of course all feces are foul-smelling),
agreed that it was Teng's.

So they all took off again after Teng. But by this time he had
crossed over the river and had had time to stir the water up,
making it all muddy. When the monkeys came along they could no
longer see where the deep and shallow places were, and since they
could not swim, they were unable to cross over. Meanwhile, Teng
had passed a rope over the river, tying it first to a tree and
instructing a squirrel on that side, "When I tell you to, you bite
through this rope. Okay, Squirrel?" Then he pulled the rope across
the stream with him and tied the other end to a tree. Having made
these preparations, Teng called to the monkeys on the other side.
"Each of you get a heavy stone to carry on your back," Teng
instructed, "and then come across on the rope." The monkeys did as
they were told. Then as they were swinging across on the rope,
Teng called out, "Everyone move to the middle of the rope." When
the monkeys had done this, Teng called to the squirrel to bite his
end of the rope while Teng cut his end. At this, the monkeys all
fell into the deep part of the river and drowned. Then Teng
fetched some firewood, roasted the monkeys, and ate them.

While Teng was sitting there eating, a tiger began to stalk
him, wanting to catch and eat him. Teng heard the tiger
stalking--pit, pat, pit, pat--and called out to him, "What are you
doing--pit, pat, pit, pat? If you want to eat, come on and eat."
The tiger was a bit disconcerted at this, but continued stalking,
going pit, pat, pit, pat. Teng called out again, "What are you
doing--pit, pat, pit, pat? If you want to eat, come on and eat."
The tiger didn't know what to do since his desire was to eat Teng.
But Teng kept inviting him to come and share the monkey meat with
him. Finally, the tiger bounded into the clearing and said,
"Alright, I'll eat." "First go down to the river and wash your
hands," Teng replied. So the tiger went down to the river and
washed his hands. But of course on the way back they got all muddy
again. Teng looked at the tiger's hands and said, "Look at your
hands! They're all muddy. Can't you even wash your hands? Here,
let me help you." So he took the tiger's paws and thrust them into

the fire. The poor tiger's paws hurt terribly, but he was unable
to do anything but just sit there and nurse them in agony.

Despite all this, Teng and the tiger soon became friends and
decided to travel together. Once they came upon a wild pig who was
digging up potatoes. Teng, who was too lazy to dig his own
potatoes, got behind the wild pig and then complained that the pig
had blinded him by throwing dirt into his eyes. He insisted that
the pig give him some potatoes since he had blinded him. So the
pig gave his potatoes to Teng. Then he told Teng to get out of his
way because he wanted to dig some more potatoes. But Teng refused
to move. When he saw that the wild pig had dug up some more
potatoes, he again complained that the pig had blinded him. He
insisted that the pig give these potatoes as well to him.

Later on Teng grew angry with the wild pig. Conceiving a plan,
he went to the tiger, saying, "Tiger, Tiger, the wild pig says he
wants to kill you!" Then he turned around and went to the wild
pig. "Pig, Pig," Teng yelled, "the tiger says he wants to kill
you!" Teng instructed the wild pig to go roll in the mud to get a
protective covering over his body. At the same time he instructed
the tiger to go out and get rattan with which to wind his whole
body in a protective covering. Then he told the tiger to spring at
the wild pig and told the wild pig to spring at the tiger. The
tiger and the wild pig made these preparations. Then the attacks
began. When the wild pig sprang at the tiger, he broke the rattan
strips, and it seemed the tiger would have the worst of the
battle. "Tiger, Tiger," shouted Teng, "Spring! Spring!" The tiger
sprang and bit the wild pig, but only got his mouth full of mud.
"For goodness sake sever his jugular vein!" Teng shouted. The
tiger made a swipe at the wild pig's jugular vein and severed it,
killing the wild pig.

Teng cut down a tree so that they could use the trunk as a
carrying pole to take the wild pig off to cook it. The heavy end
of the trunk with the branches and thorns still on it, Teng gave
to the tiger to carry. His own smaller end he carefully smoothed.
As they went along, the tiger said wearily, "Ohhh, Ohhh!" "Don't
say that," Teng retorted. "If you complain, you'll make the meat
bitter as banana blossoms, friend."

Finally, the tiger was unable to go any further. So they put
down the wild pig and decided to roast it there. Teng sent the
tiger to get fire. Pointing to the sun, he told the tiger, "Go ask
that woman for some of her fire." The tiger set off in pursuit of
the sun crying, "Wait for me, woman, wait for me!" But of course
the sun did not wait for him though he followed it far and long.
In the meantime, Teng made a fire, roasted the wild pig and ate
it, leaving just a few pieces which he put in the top of some
sections of bamboo filled with banana blossom and roasted in the
fire. When the tiger came back, tired from his unsuccessful pur-

suit of the sun, Teng gave him the sections of bamboo filled almost entirely with banana blossom and only a few pieces of meat. When the tiger expressed surprise over the taste, Teng remarked sadly, "Didn't I tell you that if you complained, you would make the meat bitter-tasting like banana blossoms?"

A day or two later the two were again without food. "What shall we eat, friend?" Teng asked the tiger. "We're without food. I guess we'll have to eat our own testicles. Tonight we'll eat mine, and tomorrow we'll eat yours. You go away while I cut mine off." But Teng had saved the testicles from the wild pig and substituted these, deceiving the tiger.

The next night he instructed the tiger to cut off his testicles for them to eat. The tiger of course was unable to do this because of the pain. Teng jeered at the cowardly tiger for being unable to do what he had done the day before. So grabbing a knife, Teng whacked off the tiger's testicles. The tiger was in such pain that he was unable to eat or do anything else. So Teng suggested that they go take a bath in the river. Teng went upstream from the tiger to bathe, but the tiger looked up while he was bathing and saw that Teng had deceived him and still had his testicles. The tiger flew into a rage and roared, "I'm going to catch Teng and eat him up."

Teng immediately flew from the tiger and ran until he came to a deserted house. Here he hid. In the house he found a nest of wasps. By the time the tiger had found the house, Teng called down to him, "What do you want to eat me for? I'll make a deal with you. I have found a valuable ancient gong in this house and I will give it to you if you won't eat me."

The tiger was tempted and came up into the dark house. Teng pointed to the wasps nest. "There it is, friend," he said, "but please don't beat it until I'm out of earshot. Otherwise I just couldn't bear to go away and leave it to you."

The tiger agreed to this, so Teng left the house, locking all the doors and windows behind him. The tiger waited the appropriate amount of time, and then struck the wasps nest. The wasps poured out and stung him. The tiger went frantically from doors to windows trying to get out. Finally, he jumped up and down on the fireplace in the center of the floor until it gave way and he fell through to the ground.

The tiger again set off after Teng, saying, "I'm going to catch Teng and eat him up." He followed Teng until he came to a place where there were two trees standing side by side. When the wind blew, these trees would rub together and go "creak, creak." Teng had crawled up into these trees and called out as the tiger approached. "Why do you want to eat me, friend? I'll make a deal with you. If you don't eat me, I'll give you my elephant here.

Don't come over now, but go up to the top of that hill there until
I leave. If you get up on the elephant now, I'll feel so sad that
I won't be able to give up my elephant."

The tiger went over to the hill as he was told, but when he
heard the "creak, creak" sound, he was very happy. He felt sure
now that there really was an elephant. Teng instructed him that
when it heard the "creak, creak" sound, the elephant was hungry.
When this happened, the tiger should put his hand into the elephant's mouth, and this would satisfy him.

After Teng had gone, the tiger went over to the trees. When he
heard the creaking sound, he put his hand into the opening between
the trees. But the wind blew them together, catching his paw
between the trees, so that he cried out in pain. Hard as he tried
he could not get his paw loose.

When the trees at last blew apart, the tiger set out again
after Teng, saying, "I'm going to catch Teng and eat him up." By
the time he caught up to Teng, Teng had come upon a large black
poisonous snake coiled up. Teng called out to the tiger, "Why do
you want to eat me, friend? I'll make a deal with you. I have
found a valuable black head cloth which I'll give you if you
promise not to eat me. It is very, very old and very precious."
The tiger could not resist this, so he promised. He went up to
where Teng waited beside the coiled black snake. "Here it is,"
Teng said, "but you mustn't put it on until I leave or I'll feel
too sad to part with it." When Teng had gone, the tiger picked up
the "cloth" and prepared to put it on his head. But of course the
snake bit him, and the tiger realized he was going to die.

Really furious now, the tiger set out again after Teng saying,
"I'm going to catch Teng and eat him up." Teng was running away
from the tiger when he came to a deep hole, stumbled, and fell
into it. It was so deep that he was unable to get out again. It
was not long before the tiger came along and found Teng there in
the hole. "What do you want to eat me for, friend?" Teng called
out. "You had better jump into this hole quick and hide. The Crai
people are burning brush and the fires will soon cover this whole
area." A turtle who had fallen in was also in the hole.

At last night fell, and Teng began to poke at the sore place
where the tiger's testicles had been. "Stop that, Teng!" the tiger
said. "What? I'm not doing anything," replied Teng. "It's the
turtle." The tiger picked up the turtle and threw it out of the
hole. But still the poking continued. "Stop that, Teng!" the tiger
repeated. Again Teng replied, "I'm not doing anything. It's the
thatch weeds that are in the hole here." So the tiger picked up
all of the thatch weeds and threw them out of the hole. But still
the poking continued. This time the tiger knew that it was Teng
doing the poking because there was nothing else in the hole. So he
picked up Teng and threw him out of the hole. Teng immediately ran

to get wood, brush, and tinder and stuffed these into the hole with the tiger, setting it afire. Thus the tiger was killed and roasted there in the hole.

Teng then went to a nearby village of the Crai people. He found the people out cutting thatch near the village. "How would you people like to have some wild buffalo meat?" he asked them. "We'd like it very much," the villagers replied. "Where is it?" "In a deep hole just a little ways from here," Teng said. "Why don't you go cut it up and bring it back?" "We don't have anyone to guard our homes while we go," they replied. "Don't worry. I'll guard your homes while you go," Teng said. So the villagers all set off for the deep hole to which Teng directed them.

But meanwhile, Teng went into the village and killed and ate all their chickens and pigs. He also killed their children and set the bodies up by the doors of the houses, propping their mouths open with sticks so that they looked like they were laughing. Then in each house he gathered the pots and dishes together, putting them together under a blanket. This resembled the form of a person sleeping all covered up. When he heard the people returning to the village, Teng climbed up into the loft of a house to hide.

When the villagers first approached their houses, they thought their children were waiting for them with joyous smiles. "What are you so happy about, children?" they called out. "There wasn't even any wild buffalo meat there. Just a tiger carcass. That fellow, Teng, tricked us saying there was wild buffalo meat out there." But when the villagers drew nearer, they saw that their children were dead, their pigs and chickens all gone. Full of grief and rage, they went into their houses where they thought they found the sleeping Teng. Grabbing heavy instruments, they beat the sleeping form, only to find that they had destroyed not Teng, but all their pots and dishes. Then they began to run wildly around the village looking for Teng. "What are you so angry about?" Teng called out from his hiding place. "If you don't want me to get away, why don't you plant stakes all along the road by the river?" Thinking this an excellent idea, the people did this. Then Teng called out, "Look! I'm up in this loft and I'm going to jump. Look up here!" Everyone rushed to the spot and looked up. Then Teng took out a package of red pepper and sprinkled it in their eyes. This blinded them so that they could not see where they were going, and running down by the water they impaled themselves on their own stakes. And so they died.

After this, Teng went on until he came to an old woman weeding her fields in the rain. "You poor thing," Teng exclaimed, "working in this rain! I really feel sorry for you, Grandmother. Go, go on home. You go home and cook some rice and fish for me, and I'll stay and finish weeding your field." The old woman was delighted and said, "It's fortunate for me that you came along, son." But when the old woman had gone, Teng went to work and pulled up every one of her rice plants. When he had finished, he went to the old woman and said, "I've finished weeding your field, Grandmother." "Oh, thank you," she replied. "Here, I've prepared some rice and fish for you." Teng sat down and ate a hearty meal. Then he said to the old woman, "In three days you go and check on the field, won't you, Grandmother?" "Oh yes," she replied. "Thank you so very much, son, for weeding the field. You have certainly been kind to help an old woman who had to work in the rain.

When he had finished eating, Teng went on his way again. He came again to another old woman carrying a heavy basket of bananas on her back. "Oh dear! You'll kill yourself trying to carry that heavy basket, Grandmother," Teng exclaimed. "Let me carry the basket. It's much too heavy for you." "Oh thank you," the old woman said. "I'd be happy for you to carry it for me." "You go on ahead, Grandmother," said Teng. "I want to stop here and bathe first. But I know where your house is, and I'll bring the basket to your house." But when the old woman had gone on home, Teng ate up all the bananas in the basket. He then threw all of the empty skins back into the basket and left one hand of the smallest bananas, which he hung over the rim of the basket. Teng carried the basket to the village and set it down outside the old woman's house. Then he went on his way.

The old woman's grandchild saw the basket and ran to get a banana. But when he looked inside, all he could see were banana skins. He ran back to tell his grandmother that he could not find any bananas. She retorted angrily, "How is it you cannot find any bananas when there is a whole basket of them out there? Have the spirits blinded you? If I find any bananas in the basket, shall I put your eyes out?" "Go ahead," the child replied. So the old woman went out, saw the hand of small bananas hanging on the rim and stabbed the child's eyes out. Then she looked into the basket and saw that Teng had eaten all of the bananas in the basket. The old woman now realized that those few tiny bananas were indeed the only ones there.

Teng by this time was well on his way out of town. He came upon a turtle which he proceeded to roast. But the turtle called out from the fire, "If you must roast me, friend, at least listen to what I say. We turtles are very skilled at playing the **ken** (a bamboo reed instrument)." Teng listened, and sure enough, he heard a faint "Sssss" sound. This, was, however, really caused by the hissing and boiling of the turtle's stomach due to the fire's heat. "Put your ear down close so that you can hear me play lovely music," said the turtle. So Teng put his ear down close to the turtle, and suddenly the turtle explosively released all the feces and stomach juices which had build up inside him. These went in Teng's ear and all over his head, causing him to fall down dead.

THE TIGER AND THE RABBIT

This story was told in Chrau by various story-
tellers and was translated by David Thomas.

One day the rabbit met the tiger and said, "Let's go collect thatch." The tiger agreed and off they went.

They cut leaves and dried them out in the sun. When the leaves were sufficiently dry, they called their friends and relatives to come and help bundle it. But when they were ready to start carrying the dried thatch home, the rabbit said, "Friend, what shall I do? I'm not big or strong enough to carry this bundle."

"If you can't carry it, Friend," the tiger replied, "just tie it onto my back."

Then as they were walking along, with the tiger carrying the large bundle of thatch on his back, the rabbit said, "Friend, I'm very cold."

"Never mind," replied the tiger, "just climb on my back. Don't worry that you're not walking. If you're cold, just climb right up on my back."

When the rabbit got seated on the tiger's back, he started pounding him.

"What are you doing, Friend?" the tiger asked.

"I'm not doing anything," the rabbbit answered. "That's just my shivering and my teeth chattering." And he went on pounding the tiger.

After a bit, the rabbit set fire to the thatch on the tiger's back and jumped off to safety. Feeling the heat, the tiger exclaimed, "Friend, what shall I do?"

"Run straight into the wind, friend," the rabbit counseled.

So the tiger ran straight into the wind, just as the rabbit had said; and the fire really began to blaze, badly burning the tiger. These burn marks are what made the tiger striped, just as he is today.

One day the tiger came across the rabbit as he was preparing traps. "Let's go now and set these traps," said the rabbit, and the tiger assented. Off they went into the forest.

The tiger set his trap on the ground, but the rabbit set his high up on a bamboo stalk. "Why did you set your trap way up there?" the tiger asked.

"This is the best way to do it," replied the rabbit. "You wait and see."

Early the next morning the rabbit stole out to the traps, where he discovered a squirrel in the tiger's trap, but nothing in his own. He took the squirrel out of the tiger's trap and put it in his own. Then he returned home.

A little later in the morning he suggested to the tiger, "Friend, let's go out and see if our traps have caught anything." When they arrived, they found the squirrel in the rabbit's trap, but nothing in the tiger's trap.

"How come you caught something and I didn't?" the tiger wanted to know.

"You put your trap on the ground; naturally it wouldn't catch anything."

"Friend, let's trade traps so that I can catch something."

"No, I don't want to," the rabbit replied. "My trap catches game and yours doesn't, so why would I want to trade with you?"

But the tiger coaxed and begged until finally the rabbit relented. The trap up in the bamboo stalk became the tiger's, and the trap on the ground became the rabbbit's.

The rabbit had lots of meat from his trap on the ground, but the tiger's trap up on the bamboo stalk didn't catch a single thing, though he went twice every day to look.

One day the rabbit decided to go out and look for edible rattan shoots. So he took an old, worn-out basket with lots of holes in it and went by the tiger's house, inviting him to go along. The tiger took a good strong back basket and went with him.

As they were going along, the tiger noticed the rabbit's basket. "Friend, why are you taking such a worn-out basket?"

"This basket of mine has holes in it so that the shoots can get out and go home ahead of me," the rabbit replied. "In such a tightly-woven basket as yours, they can't get out, and they lose some of their freshness by the time you get home and have your wife fix them."

The tiger then begged the rabbit to trade baskets with him. The rabbit finally agreed, and they traded. As they went along cutting

rattan shoots, the tiger put them into his basket, but most of
them would fall out onto the ground behind him. Quickly the rabbit
picked them up and put them into his own basket. Thus, the rabbit
filled his basket and started home well in advance of the tiger.

On reaching home, the rabbit quickly peeled the husks off the
shoots and went and dumped them in front of the tiger's house.
When the tiger arrived and saw the husks in front of his house, he
congratulated himself, "Good. My shoots have gotten here and my
wife has already begun fixing them."

He went inside, but didn't see anything. "Where are the rattan
shoots that came home?" he asked his wife.

"What shoots? I haven't seen any," replied his wife.

"You can't tell me there aren't any shoots," the tiger retorted, "because I saw the husks outside."

"Those husks? The rabbit dumped them there."

The tiger realized that he had been tricked, and swore he would
eat the rabbit the next time he saw him.

One evening the rabbit said to the tiger, "Friend, let's go
steal from the villagers." The tiger assented to this proposal,
and he took along a basket to carry the booty. But the rabbit took
along a lasso.

"Why the lasso?" the tiger asked.

"Friend, this is the way to do it," the rabbit answered. "If
things are out of your reach, you need a lasso to rope them. With
a basket like yours you can only get things near at hand."

The tiger began to beg and coax the rabbit to let him have the
lasso. Finally, the rabbit relented, and agreed to trade his lasso
for the tiger's basket.

Thus equipped, they entered a chicken house. The rabbit reached
in with his basket and scopped up the eggs easily, but the tiger
took many tries with his lasso to get just one egg.

After hiding his eggs out in the jungle, the rabbit rejoined
the tiger, and on they went to a sweet potato field where there
was a potato pit that the rabbit didn't see. So accidentally, he
fell into the pit.

"Friend," he called to the tiger, "I'm in the potato pit. I
sought shelter here because the sky is about to fall."

Alarmed, the tiger said, "If the sky is really about to fall,
then please let me come down there with you." The rabbit agreed,
and the tiger jumped down into the pit.

Soon the rabbit began to squeeze and pinch the tiger, making
him very angry. In his anger, the tiger threatened to throw the

rabbit out of the pit. But the rabbit challenged him, "Friend, you're not strong enough to do that. I dare you to try."

So the tiger picked him up and threw him out of the pit. Free at last, the rabbit filled his basket with sweet potatoes and took them home.

Then he went back to the village and called out, "There's a tiger eating up your sweet potatoes."

So all of the villagers ran out to the field and caught the tiger in the pit.

THE RABBIT AND THE TOAD

This story, in Chru, was transcribed by S. (narrator
unknown) and was translated by Eugene Fuller.

Once the rabbit asked, "How can I get some Cham rice to eat?
Every time I go to get some I fail."

"Let me teach you," offered the toad. "After I show you how,
you'll have some Cham rice to eat."

"Oh, brother toad, please teach me, because the Cham farmer has
set a trap."

"When you get caught in the trap, you must play dead and pass
gas. The Cham man will throw you away when he discovers that you
smell so rotten. Neither Cham nor Vietnamese will eat you."

So the rabbit went off, and right away got caught in the Cham's
trap. "Aha," the Cham farmer said. "Here's something for the
soup." But when he untied the rabbit from the trap, the rabbit
passed gas, as the toad had told him to do. Thinking the rabbit
was rotten, the Cham farmer threw him away.

Then the rabbit went to meet the toad. "Have you eaten any Cham
rice yet?" the toad asked.

"I've eaten some already, because I passed a lot of gas, and
the Cham threw me away. I'm really smart," the rabbit bragged,
"and I thought you said that you taught cleverness."

"Right," replied the toad. "I taught you how to get Cham rice,
but now you think you succeeded all because of your own cleverness. We'll see about that. If the Cham farmer doesn't eat you up
tomorrow, then I'm not wise."

Later, when the rabbit went to eat some more Cham rice, he was
caught again in the Cham's trap. Again the rabbit made a rotten
smell, and the Cham man exclaimed, "Oh, what a stench!"

Then the toad came up to the farmer and said, "That rabbit is
just pretending to be dead and is passing gas. That's why there is

63

a stench. You get a stick and hit him."

So the Cham got a stick and beat the rabbit until he was dead. And that's why people have eaten rabbit meat from that day until now.

THE RABBIT AND THE GAUR

This story, in Chru, was transcribed by W. (narrator
unknown) and was translated by Eugene Fuller.

From olden times the rabbit has been known to be very clever
and tricky. One day long ago, the rabbit, carrying a crossbow,
went out to shoot a gaur in the mountains. Realizing his small
size, the rabbit wondered how he would be able to shoot a big
gaur. Then he had an idea.

There are two kinds of gaur--the mountain gaur and the water
gaur. The rabbit went to the mountain gaur and said, "Oh, brother
gaur, look here. Your brother, water gaur, wants to fight you."

"All right," said the mountain gaur.

Then the rabbit went over and spoke with the water gaur. "Oh,
brother water gaur," he said, "Mountain gaur says he wants to
fight you, and that it will be a fight to the finish."

"All right," agreed the water gaur.

The rabbit arranged for them to meet each other on the mountain
the very next day. Then he went home. Early the next morning he
left with his crossbow and arrows and arrived at the mountain
before noon. He climbed to the top of a tree and a moment later
the mountain gaur and the water gaur arrived and began fighting.

The rabbit stayed up in the tree, watching. Fiercely the two
gaurs fought each other, breaking trees and even rocks. In the
end, the water gaur lost, and so he died. Then the mountain gaur
returned to his mountain.

The rabbit came down from the tree, took an arrow, and stuck it
into the water gaur. He told everyone that he had shot it. Thus,
the rabbit got his gaur meat.

65

THE TIGER AND THE SNAIL

This story was told in Pacoh by A.
and was translated by Saundra Watson.

Once there was a tiger who wandered about from place to place. He was crazed with hunger and was hunting deer or any other animal, but he could not find anything to eat.

Then the tiger came to the water, where he met a snail crawling along. "Oh, I'm so hungry that I could eat a snail!" the tiger said.

"What's that?" the snail exclaimed. "Eat me? That's not a good idea!" And he repeated, "Eat me? That's not a good idea at all!"

"Let's race to that place over there," challenged the tiger. "If I get there before you do, I will eat you. But if you arrive before I do, I will not eat you."

So the snail agreed. "If I am last, you may eat me. I will allow it. But if I am not last, you must keep your word. I will not allow you to eat me."

The tiger began to run. He ran and ran a very long way, every now and again, calling out, "Oh, snail!"

But, of course, there was always a snail in every stream who answered, "Here I am, out ahead." However much the tiger ran, the snail was always ahead of him. Whenever the tiger came to a stream, the snail was already there. So obviously, the tiger lost the race.

He was fiercely angry over being defeated, and picking up the snail, the tiger bit down hard. The tiger cried out in pain. "I lose to you," he finally conceded. I will not try to eat you again."

HRIT AND THE RABBIT

This story was told in Bahnar by Mr. B
and was translated by John Banker.

Hrit and the rabbit were very good friends. On the day this story begins, the rabbit had heard Hrit say he was going out to have some fun.

Meanwhile, the rabbit hopped over to Mrs. Hen Feather's for a visit. He stood outside and called, "Oh, Grandmother, is your house taboo or not?"

"Who's there?" she answered.

"I'm here," the rabbit replied.

"Come on up and visit, Grandchild," she invited him. So the rabbit went up, and asked Mrs. Hen Feather where Hrit had gone.

"He's gone out somewhere to have some fun, I guess," she said.

Sitting there, the rabbit began to feel tired. He said to Mrs. Hen Feather, "Grandma, do you want to weave a loincloth for me?"

"If you'd like me to, I'll weave you one."

"How many days will it take?"

"In three days it will be finished."

"Then do it quickly, okay?" the rabbit pleaded. "I'll pull weeds for you."

So Mrs. Hen Feather wove the loincloth for the rabbit. When she was just about finished, Hrit came over. "Who are you weaving that for?" he asked.

"For your friend, the rabbit," she replied.

Just then the rabbit came back from the field and asked her if she had finished yet.

"Almost finished," she answered.

67

"Do it quickly. I have pulled out almost all of the weeds already."

Then the rabbit returned to the field to pull out more weeds. But instead, he pulled out all the rice and left the weeds.

Later, Mrs. Hen Feather asked him, "What have you been pulling up in the field?"

"I've been pulling yeeds and leaving wice," the rabbit replied.

"What have you been doing, really? Have you truly been pulling out weeds?"

"I've been pulling yeeds and leaving wice."

Then Mrs. Hen Feather realized that "pulling yeeds and leaving wice" meant pulling rice and leaving weeds, so she confronted the rabbit.

"That means that you probably have been pulling out rice and leaving weeds."

"Oh no," the rabbit protested. "Let's go and see."

When they got to the field, Mrs. Hen Feather saw that the rabbit had indeed pulled out all of the rice.

"Oh, Rabbit, you have used me badly; but why?"

Without waiting for an answer, she immediately grabbed a stick and hit the rabbit.

The rabbit ran back to the house with Mrs. Hen Feather in pursuit. "Hrit, hit the rabbit there," she called, still far from the house.

But Hrit didn't understand, so the rabbit said, "She told us to hurry and roast the big pig. She said that if we don't do it right now, when she gets here she will beat us to death."

Mrs. Hen Feather came on running from the field, continuing to yell for Hrit to hit the rabbit. This time Hrit understood, so he said, "There. Mrs. Hen Feather told me to hit you."

"Oh, no, you're mistaken, Hrit. She said that she wanted to hit us because we're not hurrying to roast the pig."

The rabbit was afraid of the beating Mrs. Hen Feather would give him when she caught up to him, so he quickly stabbed the thigh of the pig, grabbed Hrit and ran, saying that Mrs. Hen Feather would beat them both.

On and on they ran, with Mrs. Hen Feather chasing after them, axe in hand. Finally, they sought shelter in a hollow tree. Being small, the rabbit climbed up high, while Hrit stayed below.

Mrs. Hen Feather found their hiding place, and commanded the rabbit, "Come on out, Rabbit."

But Hrit replied, "It's Hrit here, Grandma."

But Mrs. Hen Feather didn't believe him. So when he came out of the hollow tree, she hit him hard, and he died. It was her grandson, Hrit.

"Oh, Grandchild, you have died," she mourned. "Oh, my grandchild is dead."

For two days she stayed there, mourning.

During this time, the rabbit began to feel very hungry, so he at last climbed out of the hollow tree. Mrs. Hen Feather caught him, and carried both him and Hrit back to the house.

The rabbit also mourned for his friend Hrit.

Later the rabbit overheard Mrs. Hen Feather say she wanted to sell him to Mr. Roh. So quickly the rabbit went over to Mr. Roh, and offered, "Would you like to buy a person?"

"Where did you get this person?" Mr. Roh asked.

"She's a very beautiful young woman, who wants to marry me, but I don't like her. Therefore, I told her that she should live with you. You are rich with many water buffalo and cattle. Now she wants to live with you. If you want her, then you may take her--it's all right with me."

Mr. Roh felt a thrill in his heart as the rabbit told him this. "Tomorrow you bring her here to me," he instructed the rabbit.

"I will," the rabbit promised. Immediately he went back to Mrs. Hen Feather's house.

The next day Mrs. Hen Feather asked the rabbit to go with her for a visit to Mr. Roh's. They walked together until they were near his village, and then the rabbit excused himself. "I really need to go over there for a minute," he told Mrs. Hen Feather.

Then he ran off and talked to Mr. Roh, who was ready with a present of two water buffalo--a white one and a black one--and one small gong.

"Before you go to get this beautiful young woman, wait until you hear me gonging far from here," the rabbit said. "Listen to me beat the gong all the way until you can't hear anymore; then you go get her."

The rabbit went on his way, all the time beating the gong: ping, ping, ping. Mr. Roh listened until he couldn't hear the gong anymore. Then he said to his servants and slaves, "Let's go and get this one that the rabbit has been talking about."

But before leaving, Mr. Roh went and got all dressed up. Then they went out and met Mrs. Hen Feather!

"Have you seen that woman that the rabbit told me was so beautiful and sold to me for two water buffalo?" he asked her.

Mrs. Hen Feather burst out crying in anger, "I am the one, Roh. I said that I wanted to sell him, but instead he has sold me!"

Roh was also very angry because the rabbit had lied and sold him Mrs. Hen Feather. Then Mrs. Hen Feather told Mr. Roh all about the rice pulling and about Hrit's death.

"I'm very angry with him; he continually tells lies. Now when I was going to sell him, he sells me instead!"

Together Mrs. Hen Feather and Mr. Roh looked for the rabbit, but they couldn't find a trace of him. The rabbit and all the things he'd cheated Mr. Roh to get were gone.

But the rabbit was lonely. He just herded his carabao until he was about to go crazy. Poor rabbit had no friends.

"White and black carabao," he said, "today I will tie you far from each other."

Then when the sun was about to go down, he said to the black buffalo, "Black buffalo, look at that white carabao! He's cursing you, inviting you to fight him. Look at him sharpening his horns and stomping the earth furiously! He's just spoiling for a fight."

Then the rabbit went over and said the same things to the white buffalo. That was all the encouragement the two of them needed. They immediately began to fight each other.

The rabbit sat on his haunches in the top of a tree, watching the action. The water buffalos fought and fought until they both died. Sad and lonely, the rabbit kept sitting there in the tree.

Then after a while, he saw a tiger coming along. The tiger was just about to eat the slain water buffalo when the rabbit called out, "Hey mister, are you stealing my water buffalo."

The rabbit scrambled down from the tree, saying, "What a pity! The tiger doesn't have anything to eat. Such a pity."

So the tiger asked the rabbit if he could eat some of the water buffalo, and the rabbit took pity on him. He told the tiger to go get some fire, pointing to the sun which was about to set. The tiger went off to get the setting sun.

When he returned, the tiger and the rabbit roasted the water buffalo. Then the rabbit instructed the tiger to weave a basket. When he had finished, the rabbit took the basket and tied it to a root of a banyan tree very securely. Then he cut up the water buffalo bones and put them in the bottom of the basket. On top of the bones he placed stones, and on the very top, he put some meat.

They were just about ready to eat when the rabbit told the
tiger to finish cutting off the meat and filling the basket while
he went over to tiger's house to get some salt. Upon arriving at
tiger's house, the rabbit tied up the tiger's wife and sewed her
mouth shut. He then set spikes under the porch and cut the porch
posts almost through in many places.

This done, the rabbit returned to the tiger and told him to
carry the basket back to the house. The tiger strained on the
basket once, and then again so hard that the strap broke and he
cut his shoulder. But finally he managed to lug the heavy basket
home.

"Oh wife," the tiger called, "come and open the door for me."

But the tiger's wife only answered, "Mmmmm."

The tiger walked up on the porch. Crunch, crunch bang--and he
fell down right on the spikes. He got up and went into the house
only to find that his wife was also in dire straits.

"Who sewed up your mouth?" he demanded.

"The rabbit did it," she replied when her husband had undone
the sewing.

Now the tiger was really angry with the rabbit. Piece by piece
he took out the meat, lean meat first, and then all the bones and
stones. He told his wife how despicable the rabbit was.

"I thought he had given me all meat, but most of it was stones
and bones, and that's why it was so hard to carry. Just wait until
I get my hands on that rabbit! I'll eat him up in a minute."

The tiger was very angry because he had carried the heavy
basket, largely full of useless stones and bones, had been wounded
in the process, and his wife had been hurt--all on account of the
crafty rabbit.

Several days later, the tiger came upon the rabbit tapping on a
bumblebee's hive. "Be careful," the tiger warned. "I'm very angry
because you used me very badly. Now I'm going to eat you up."

"You say you want to eat me," the rabbit answered. "It would be
better if you took this musical instrument handed down from my
grandmother and grandfather."

"Why? Does it make good music?" the tiger asked.

"Just listen," the rabbit said. And he tapped slowly on the
hive. "Poong, poong; we, we."

"It is very pleasant," the tiger agreed. "Just let me have it
and I won't eat you."

"But you still want to hit me," the rabbit replied. "So don't do anything until you hear me far away. Wait until you can no longer hear the sound of this gong I'm going to beat." So the tiger listened until he could no longer hear the sound of the rabbit's gong. Then he hit the beehive hard. "Poong, poong, we, we." Then he hit it very hard again, this time making a hole in it. Out came the bumblebees by the droves. They stung the tiger all over his face, until it was completely swollen.

Ignoring his injuries for the moment, the tiger ran after the rabbit and found him sitting hear a creaking tree, listening. Just as the tiger was about to pounce on the rabbit, the rabbit spoke.

"Who do you want to pounce upon? If you're angry with some rabbit, what kind is it? Are you looking for a meadow rabbit or a woods rabbit?"

"I'm looking for a meadow rabbit," replied the tiger.

"Oh, I'm not a meadow rabbit. I'm a woods rabbit,"

"Then why have you been sitting here all this time?" the tiger wanted to know.

"Why have I been sitting here? I've been listening to this one-stringed violin that belonged to my grandmother and grandfather."

The tiger listened, too. "It truly is a pleasant sound," he agreed.

"Would you like to buy it? How much will you give me? On second thought, I can't sell it; it's too dear to me. It was bequeathed to me by my grandparents, and it's the only one like it in the whole world. No, I can't sell it. But if you would like to listen, I'll let you. But you must stick out your tongue between those two trees. Oh, you just can't imagine how beautiful it will be!"

When the rabbit had walked away, the tiger stuck out his tongue between the two trees. Immediately the trees squeezed together and cut the tiger's tongue in two.

"Yeeeaauu!" he yelled so loudly that he could be heard all through the mountains.

The rabbit heard the cries of the tiger, and retorted, "There! You wanted to eat me, but now your tongue is cut in two. Does it still hurt?"

The rabbit thought very hard, with his ears standing straight up. Then he said, "Well, the tiger is still alive, but if he meets me again, he will surely die."

Then the rabbit hopped off to a place where there was a trap set. Soon he saw the familiar, evil-looking face with a cut tongue coming down the trail.

"Come here, Sir. Come here," the rabbit called.

The rabbit went first, ahead of the tiger, cautiously and slowly moving along. But the tiger, in rage and pain, came plunging and thrashing all over the place. Soon they came to the place where the trap was, and the tiger fell in the trap. He was caught fast, unable to get out.

"There!" the rabbit taunted. "You wanted to eat me. Well, now I'm going to tell the owner of the trap."

"Oh, Grandchild," the tiger pleaded, shaking all over, "pity me a little and I'll pay you, okay?"

But the rabbit wouldn't agree. Off he went with a smirk on his face to the village to seek the owner of the trap.

"People, you have a trap. Come and look at it."

The people went to see the trap and found the tiger already dead. They carried him back to their houses and roasted and ate him.

And the rabbit had peace because the tiger was dead.

MR. COUNTLESS-WARTS

This story, told in Black Tai by Mr. Q.,
a sixty-eight-year-old grandfather,
was translated by Jay Fippinger.

Once upon a time, there was a married couple who had a baby boy. This baby did not have clear skin like that of a normal child. Rather, from the time he was born, his whole body was covered with pimples and warts. So people called him Countless Warts. While he was still quite young, his parents died.

After he grew up, Mr. Countless Warts built a house deep in the forest, where he lived all by himself. He preferred not to live among other people because he was shy and ashamed. Not only was his body different from other people's, being completely covered with pimples and warts, but he also had an unpleasant odor. So Mr. Countless Warts withdrew from society and lived all alone in the forest.

One day Mr. Countless Warts took a knife and an axe and went to find wood suitable to build himself a pig pen and a chicken coop. As he was going along, he noticed a tangerine tree from which hung a single, large, succulent piece of fruit. Wanting very much to taste this beautiful tangerine, Mr. Countless Warts cut a forked stick and tried to pluck it from the tree. But the tree was too tall, so the stick couldn't reach it. Nevertheless, he kept trying, and at last the tangerine fell down. Plop! Right into his eye! In his pain and anger, he wasn't able to eat it. Instead, he kept rubbing his eye until it cleared up. Then he picked up the fruit, rubbed it on his body, and, in anger and annoyance, hurled it into the river without so much as tasting it.

So Mr. Countless Warts returned to his home in the forest and continued to live as before. Meanwhile, the tangerine floated down the river, until it came to the bathing spot of a young princess, the ruler's youngest child. At midday, when she went down to the river to bathe, the princess noticed the tangerine drifting along. She saw that the fruit was very lovely, so she took it up to examine it. It was still good, not spoiled. She peeled it; it had a pleasant smell. And when she tasted it, she found it deliciously

74

sweet. So the princess ate it all up. Then she finished bathing and went home.

The princess still lived with her parents. No one had yet proposed to her nor come to do brideservice. She was still a virgin, unmarried and chaste. And yet she became pregnant. As her abdomen grew larger and larger, her parents also came to realize her condition.

"Who came and slept with you, child, seeing that now you are pregnant? Tell us truthfully what happened and we will give you in marriage to that man, whoever he is. We won't try to dissuade you. You will live together as man and wife and the child will be his."

But the ruler's daughter replied, "No one has come and slept with me! I have had no lovers! I've just been living here with you."

So they waited. As the weeks passed, it became obvious that the princess was indeed pregnant. The movement in her abdomen could only be that of a baby. Her parents confronted her again.

"Don't try to hide anything from us. We won't scold you or be angry with you. Whatever happened, tell us about it truthfully. It's all right. Remember what we told you."

"I haven't deceived you," the princess protested. "The truth is that no one has come and slept with me."

Nine months passed, and the time came for the ruler's daughter to give birth. A beautiful baby boy was born to her. When he was eight months old, her parents came to her once more.

"You say that no one has come and slept with you," they said. "How is it, then, that you have had a baby?"

"I don't know," the princess replied. "I don't know who the father could be. I've had this child as a virgin; that's all there is to tell."

"All right, then," her parents said, "That's good enough for us. We will make a proclamation throughout the realm, summoning all the men from sixteen to forth-five years of age. They will all come together in the palace courtyard, and I will ask them, 'Whose child is this?' You and your child will be in the middle, but at that moment, you will release the baby to crawl to whomever he will. That man, whomever the baby crawls to, will become the father of the child. It doesn't matter whether he is good or bad, rich or poor; he cannot refuse. Will you agree to this plan?"

"I'm very willing to have it as you have said," the princess assented. "I'm happy to hear of your plan and will be willing to take the man that the baby chooses as my husband. Only give the command, and he will become the baby's father and my husband. This is the way my destiny is being revealed, and I welcome it."

So the ruler issued a proclamation. At a certain date and time all the men from sixteen through forth-five were to gather at the ruler's house. Anyone who dared disobey would be arrested. On the appointed day, therefore, everyone gathered together--everyone, that is, with the exception of Mr. Countless Warts. Because of his very unattractive appearance, with pimples all over his body, he was ashamed to mix with other people. So he stayed home instead of going to the meeting.

But someone reported his absence to the ruler, "That man who lives by himself in the forest--Mr. Countless Warts they call him--he's only forty-five years old, but he hasn't come."

Right away, then, the ruler dispatched someone to fetch Mr. Countless Warts to the gathering. They arrested him, but he came along only reluctantly, angry, and sobbing. He was very poor and he feared other people. Being so poor, he had had nothing with which to develop his home, so there was nothing in his house that would serve as a gift. All he had were a few pepper plants and eggplants he had grown to eat. So, before leaving, he yanked off one of the eggplants and took it with him.

Everyone who had gathered in the palace courtyard had brought something. Joint gifts were not permitted, so each person had brought something different. What a variety of things there were: stringed instruments, sugar, clocks, and wind instruments! (While they waited, some of them blew on the wind instruments, just for fun.) No one could come empty-handed, so into this impressive array of gifts, Mr. Countless Warts came bearing the only thing he had to offer--an eggplant. Poor as he was, he didn't have anything else to give.

Upon arriving, Mr. Countless Warts sat down and heard the ruler announce, "My daughter has had a child, though she says that she is still a virgin. Even though no one has had relations with her, she has had a child. Therefore, I made the proclamation that every male aged sixteen through forty-five should gather here today. Here are my daughter and her son. Now she will let him go to crawl to whomever he will. That person will henceforth be the child's father, and I will give him my daughter to be his wife. I want you all to take heed and not to refuse."

At that, all the men started to make merry, plucking their stringed instruments, blowing their wind instruments, and holding out all sorts of attractive things. But Mr. Countless Warts, having only his eggplant, stayed outside the crowd.

Then the princess released her child. The baby crawled right outside the group to Mr. Countless Warts, took the eggplant, and sat in his lap. Mr. Countless Warts was frightened. He was afraid that the ruler would kill him. He was foul-smelling and poor; how could he provide for other people's children? So he tried to push the child off his lap, but the boy wouldn't budge. Mr. Countless Warts kept trying to refuse him by pushing him off his lap, but the child simply curled up and went to sleep, right on his lap!

After waiting about fifteen minutes, the ruler proclaimed to the crowd, "That man is the child's father. All of you bear witness that I now commit my daughter to him to be his wife. No one else shall have her. Only he will be her husband, and they will form a family."

Thus it happened that the princess was given to Mr. Countless Warts in marriage. At first, he was afraid and tried to refuse, but the ruler insisted. The princess remembered what her parents had said, and obeyed their instructions. After the ruler and his wife had committed their daughter to him, Mr. Countless Warts took her to live with him in his house in the forest.

The ruler's parting words to him were, "You are now taking my daughter with you. Even though you are poor now, don't let your wife and son become destitute. You must see to it that they have food and a home. Don't be lazy, but work hard to provide food and drink for them. It would be a great pity for them to go hungry."

Mr. Countless Warts heeded the words of his father-in-law. After discussing the matter with his wife, they went together to clear a dry field in the forest. In three days, they had finished chopping down the trees, but on the fourth day, when Mr. Countless Warts went out to look at the field, all of the trees were standing again! There wasn't a single tree still lying down.

He ran back to tell his wife what had happened. "All of the trees that we chopped down are standing upright again! We worked, chopping for three days, and now on the fourth day, all of the trees are standing up in their places. This is very strange: how could it have happened, my wife and child?"

As the couple talked it over, his wife came up with a plan. "Tomorrow morning," she suggested, "go early over to the field. I'll fix food for you to take along; save enough from your lunch for supper, too. Then, after you have chopped all day as usual, hide yourself outside the field and watch. You will then be able to see what happens to make the trees you've just cut stand upright again. Indeed, it is very strange!"

So Mr. Countless Warts followed the plan that his wife had suggested. All day he worked, chopping trees. When it was time to quit, he left the field as if he were going home, but instead, he back-tracked, hid beside the field, and watched. In a little while, three monkeys appeared. One of the monkeys was very large, as big as a human being. The other two were smaller and were carrying a gong with nine nodes, striking it as they went. Each node they struck made a beautiful sound.

When they came to the trees that Mr. Countless Warts had just chopped down, the big monkey pointed at them and told the smaller ones to strike the gong. They struck a node, and all the trees stood upright.

"So that's what's been happening!" Mr. Countless Warts observed. "The monkey is the one doing this to me. No matter how many trees I cut, he puts them all back up." Again taking his wife's advice, he took a knife, ran out of his hiding place, and captured the monkey. With a strangle-hold on its neck, he was about to slash it with his knife, when the monkey called out, "Don't kill me, I beg you! If you spare my life, I'll do something very beneficial for you."

"Beneficial, ha!" Mr. Countless Warts retorted. "I cut down trees, and you raise them up. I need a field to grow things for my wife and child, who are about to starve. Yet you come and spoil it all for me. Why?"

"You don't understand," the monkey replied. "Let me show you."

"Okay, you show me," Mr. Countless Warts agreed. "What happens when you strike those nine nodes of the gong?"

So the monkey struck one node to make all of the trees fall over, and they did.

"Now strike a node so that they'll come back upright," commanded Mr. Countless Warts.

The monkey struck another node, and all of the trees returned to upright positions. Mr. Countless Warts began to see that the gong had great possibilities.

"Could you strike a node that would make all these warts disappear, so that I would be like other people?" he asked.

"I could," replied the monkey. With that, he struck the gong, and all the warts disappeared. Mr. Countless Warts was completely well! His body was completely clear of any blemish.

Then he forgave the monkey, saying, "Now I won't kill you, but release you, on one condition. You must give me this gong and instruct me how to use it. Tell me what each of the nine nodes is for."

"This one causes death," the monkey replied, and this one prevents death. This one causes barren places to be inhabited, and this other one produces rice and meat to eat. This one makes prosperous cities and everything that goes with them: citizens, rich fields and a bountiful life for all the inhabitants ..."

So the monkey went on, until the man had learned it all. Then, taking the gong, he let the monkey go free. By the time the man returned home, it was dark. He called out to his wife and child to open the door for him.

But his wife didn't trust the strange voice she heard. When he had been covered all over with pimples and warts, his voice had been very harsh. But now it was resonant and beautiful, not at all like the voice she knew as her husband's. So she answered, "I know you must be an imposter. Don't lie to me. You can't be my husband. Though a child of royalty, I married into poverty. My husband is but a poor working man and he comes to eat here. Don't you take me from him."

"Oh, no," protested her husband. "I've merely done what you said. When we were talking together, you suggested that I go watch the clearing. As I did so, I spied some monkeys with a gong that they could strike either to make the trees stand upright or to fall down again. So I captured them, and made them strike the gong near my body for all the warts to disappear. Now I've come home, with a completely clear body."

But his wife was still incredulous. Give me your hand," she said, "so I can feel it." Opening the door no more than a crack, she allowed him to put his hand inside. When she felt how smooth it was, she exclaimed, "That's not my husband's hand! But if you really are my husband and have that gong still with you, can you strike one of the nodes to bring back the warts?"

"All right," he agreed.

Then he struck the gong to make the countless warts return, and stretched out his hand for his wife to hold. When she took hold of it, feeling again the familiar warts and pimples, she exclaimed, "Truly, this is my husband! What you've said is true. Now strike the gong again, so that the warts and pimples will disappear once more."

Then she opened the door to her clear-skinned husband. They went in together, talking happily. "That monkey came, intending to harm us," the husband said. "But now he's relinquished to us his gong with the nine nodes. Never more will we want for anything to eat. If we strike this node, there will be inhabited lands and citizens, friends, and relatives. If we strike this other node, there will be oxen and buffalo, and rich wet and dry fields. This other node can create government and military posts, where people live together in harmony and bounty."

All of this came about because God sent that princess on an assignment. Because she had faith, listened, and obeyed whatever her parents told her to do, it went well with her. She obtained houses, lands, and riches, and once more lived in inhabited areas. Both she and her husband, the former 'Mr. Countless Warts', enjoyed business rank and were very happy.

CHOT CANIET

This story was told in Chrau by Mr. G.P.S.,
an old man and respected story teller,
and was translated by Dorothy Thomas.

There once was a man named Chot Caniet. His hands were itchy, his feet were itchy: he was itchy and scratchy all over.

One day Chot Caniet went to scoop up some water, and in the process, caught a catfish. He went home and put it out to dry in the front yard. Just then a crow appeared from nowhere, cawed, and grabbed the fish.

Later, the king's daughter found the fish on her doorstep. She picked it up and ate it. Soon she discovered that she was pregnant. What was she to do?

Her father noticed that her dietary habits had changed. "Why are you eating so differently from what you usually do?" he asked.

"It's nothing," she answered. "It's just that I sometimes crave this and that. Lately I crave fruits."

"I'm afraid you've been up to something," said her father.

"Oh, no, father, may I drop dead if there has been anything. If I wanted anyone without your permission, you would chop my head off. But I am always honest with you and Mother, and truthfully, I tell you that I haven't done what you say. I have always done what you have taught me; always I have behaved in accordance with how you raised me, and truly I thank you for the instructions you gave me. What can I say? One day I became pregnant, but there weren't any men around. It was the day that a crow came in from somewhere, carrying a catfish in its mouth. The fish fell at my doorway, I ate it, and after that I missed my period. I've missed it for two months now. Now, Mother, explain it if you can, and tell me what I should do. My life is in your and father's hands, but I swear that I have been telling you the truth. I have never wavered to the left or right in my obedience to you."

The parents and the relatives talked over the situation to decide what should be done. They decided to find out who was responsible for their daughter's pregnancy.

"Ask whomever you will," the princess said, "but I'm telling you the truth. Why would I want anybody? You have taken good care of me, Mother and Father, so why would I cause you trouble? How could I bring trouble on all my aunts and uncles and cousins? You have always given me enough to eat and been very good to me, so why would I bring disgrace on the family, as you say? I just got pregnant accidentally, but if you want to punish me, I will submit to it."

"But I swear, may I drop dead if I would intentionally bring disgrace on my family! I raise my hand to heaven and say that I would never want that! Test me for the truth, if you want. But believe me when I say that since I've reached puberty, no man has had contact with me. All I did was to eat a catfish that fell kerplunk at my door. I don't know where the fish came from, but after I ate it, I missed my period. That's all I have to say. Now I've explained the whole thing truthfully."

"Well, I suppose that's all there is to be said. You're sure about it? Very well, your mother and I have been discussing what should be done, and we've come to a decision. I'm going to invite everyone to come together in one place. By 'everyone' I mean all the officials, relatives, neighbors, and ordinary citizens. I'll include all the village chiefs, and assistants from every town and village, as well as all the provincial officials. Everybody will gather together in one place."

At the king's invitation, everyone began to arrive at the appointed time. There were officials with mandarin caps and those with long flowing pants and robes, and there was Mr. Chot Caniet, who just slept in the ashes of the kitchen fire. Everyone from everywhere aspired to the hand of the princess, but only the king could decide who would have her.

Now, by this time, the baby had already been born, so the king instructed his daughter to give the child some betel and tobacco. "Then," he said, "we'll see which one the child gives them to. That man will be the baby's father. It makes no difference who the man is--important or not, a village chief or an ordinary person--anybody at all."

At the big gathering Chot Caniet was sitting at the sidelines by the fire. (I tell you, by the eye of a duck, old Chot Caniet couldn't do anything! He just lived out in the open, by the fire and drying racks). The child went right to Chot Caniet and said, "Here, Father, have some tobacco."

But Chot Caniet protested, "Why are you giving that to me, little one? Don't you know that I can't go anywhere and can't do anything? I can't sit still, because I always have to itch and scratch. I just sleep out in the open, next to the fire, and get covered with ashes and splashed with boiling water. So you shouldn't be giving those things to me."

Everyone there saw what had happened. There they were--all the important people, village chiefs, provincial chiefs, and so on--each one wanting very much to marry the king's daughter, but they couldn't. And they watched the little child carry the betel to Chot Caniet and say, "Here's some tobacco and betel, Father."

They also heard Chot Caniet's reply, "I'm just the Itchy Man. You can't bring the tobacco and betel to me."

When the king saw what had transpired, he called Chot Caniet to come up and talk with him. Chot Caniet went to the king and explained, "Here is the truth, Grandfather. Some time ago, I went to get water, and I caught a catfish. When I got back home, I had no salt, so I just urinated on the fish and put it out to dry. While it was drying, a crow came--I have no idea from where--and carried the fish away in its mouth. I don't know where it flew to after that. That's the whole story."

After listening to Chot Caniet's story, the king asked his daughter, "What do you have to say, child?"

"The fish fell at our house, and I ate it and immediately missed a period. You can scold me and beat me, but the truth is that I haven't been near Chot Caniet. He's so itchy and scratchy, how could I get near him, or he to me? The simple truth is that I ate a fish and became pregnant."

"Now what will we do?" the king mused. "It has been your fate, this miracle. You and he are both lazy, and you ate the semen and got pregnant. All right, I give my consent to your marriage."

"Oh, Father, if you and mother say so, your child won't argue. But I certainly wish that I hadn't eaten that catfish."

"But you did eat the catfish, so there's no use arguing. What can we do? Be happy with your lot; don't argue. I invited all the relatives and important people from all of the towns and villages to come here, but not one of them had anything to do with causing the life of your child. So now it's just you and Chot Caniet. You must find a place to live and work with him now."

"Father, Father, what can I do? I can't argue with my mother and father."

Then Chot Caniet spoke out: "Oh, Mother, I'm itchy and scratchy, and I sleep by the fire and drying racks. How ever did I get myself into this? How could I possibly have come near to the king's child? It must be my destiny; it had to happen this way."

"Friend," the king's wife admonished, "take good care of your wife and child, hear?"

"Yes, ma'am, I will," Chot Caniet promised.

Then the parents gave them some rice and a pair of buffalo for their journey, and they set out. But Chot Caniet was so itchy and scratchy that he couldn't even drive a cart. So his wife drove about half way to their destination, then stopped.

"We've come a long way," Chot Caniet said. "Let's just stay here for awhile. We'll unhitch the buffalo and leave them here to graze at the edge of the jungle. There's grass here for them to eat."

So Chot Caniet and his wife stayed there one night, two nights, three nights .... After the fifth night, he said to his wife, "What are we going to do? We are really hard up, you know. But I have an idea. Tomorrow morning, you cook me some rice early, and let me go out for a change and a rest from this place.

"Where can you go? You're so itchy and scratchy!"

But Chot Caniet was not dissuaded. He took his walking stick and went out to look at the jungle. Clunk, clunk, clunk, went his walking stick, as he walked along, carrying a rock, a machete, and a bag of cooked rice. Finally, he came to a place and made beginning efforts to clear a field. But, being so itchy and scratchy, he chopped only haphazardly; all he managed to clear was a space one meter long--only one armspan. Then it was late, so he went home.

His wife greeted him by saying, "You've come home very late."

"I could hardly make it home," he replied. "You see, I cut down two or three trees."

Meanwhile, some monkeys appeared at the site that Chot Caniet had cleared in the jungle. "Friends," one of them shouted, "who has messed up our jungle here? Surely the sky won't like it."

The monkey leader then commanded, "Stand up, O trees." Key-yoong, the trees stood up.

Early in the morning, Chot Caniet told his wife, "Cook me some rice."

"Where did you go yesterday?" she asked.

"Oh, I went looking for bees, fish, clams, and snails."

"Clams and snails? I didn't see you bring any home."

"Well, I don't hunt very systematically--just sort of haphazardly, according to my itches and scratches. I'm crazy."

They talked like that for awhile, and in the end, his wife cooked him some rice, and off he went once more into the jungle.

This time he cut three areas for a field, resting only at noon to sharpen his knife on a big tree. At dusk, he returned home. Every day he followed the same schedule, but he didn't tell his wife what he was doing. His wife would ask him, "Why do you come home every day when it is so dark?"

But he would evade her inquiries by replying, "Oh, what can I do? I just go and do things and eat."

"How can you work?" his wife persisted. "You're all itchy and scratchy. You should come home early. Aren't you afraid of returning home so late?"

"No, I'm not afraid. And the buffalo and the cart of rice that your father and mother gave us are your responsibility. You must take care of them."

"That cart of rice is dwindling every day. And yet you keep going out, but not doing anything."

"How am I supposed to get ahead?" he argued. "I go look for greens and grasses, rattan and vines, but nothing much comes of it. It just doesn't work out."

For two or three days he and his wife continued their discussion along those lines. Meanwhile, each day she made rice, and each day he went out to chop more trees. Each day when he arrived at the clearing, however, he would find that the trees were still standing. It was very provoking. One morning, he became very angry about the situation and decided to stay home. He took a pestle, a pole, a mallet, and a whip and did incantations over them. (While he was doing the incantations, the thought came to him: since he possessed supernatural powers, why was he itchy and scratchy? He decided that someone must have made him like that.) When he had finished, he set the whip, pole, and other things in readiness. Then he sat quietly the rest of the day, not saying anything.

In the morning, he spoke again to his wife. "Cook me some rice very early, okay? In fact, cook it in the middle of the night."

"You're crazy," she replied. "Where are you going to go at midnight? It's bad enough that you go out early all the time when the cock crows, but now you want to go out at midnight. There's no sense in it."

"Enough," replied Chot Caniet. "You get the rice ready, and it will get light soon enough, gradually. Now get going."

When he spoke like that, his wife ran right away to obey him. There was no fish or meat of any kind--not even any red peppers-- so she cooked just the rice, with a chunk of salt. That's all there was.

Chot Caniet took the food his wife had prepared and his now-enchanted implements and set off. He reached a patch of thatching grass, hid himself there, and waited.

Soon he heard the voice of a monkey. "Friends, who has been messing up our jungle? Look, it's terrible!"

Chot Caniet stayed hidden and didn't say anything.

Then the monkey leader commanded, "Stand up, stand up, trees." And all the trees stood up.

Chot Caniet came out of hiding and called to them, "So, friends, you've been responsible for all of this, eh? Here I am, itchy and scratchy and lame, trying hard to make a field, and you undo everything. I chop down trees, and you make them stand up again. Today I've caught you in the act!"

With this, he spoke to his pestle and pole saying, "Enough, enough, friends." (Everything is opposite in the spirit world, so "enough" really means "beat" and vice versa.) So the pole went out and began to beat on the monkey. Crash, bang. It beat on him hard.

Soon the monkey cried, "Stop, friend, stop!"

Chot Caniet then commanded, "Beat." Immediately, the pole ceased its beating. "Now what?" Chot Caniet asked.

"Let me bring things forth for you," the monkey offered. And he brought forth all manner of dangerous things--knives, bushhooks, etc.

So Chot Caniet spoke again to his implements, "Enough, friends, enough." All of them began beating on the hands and feet of the monkeys. They beat and beat, until the monkeys were almost dead.

Finally, one of the monkeys called out, "Wait, friend, wait."

So Chot Caniet said to his sticks, "Beat, friends." and there was no more beating.

The monkey offered to bring forth other things. "What shall I do for you, friend? Let me bring forth buffalo and gongs, rice fields and paddies. You'll be rich. I can also bring forth houses of silver, two-storied houses, tiled houses, tall houses--any kind you want--and the people to fill them. I can give you animals--cattle and buffalo, horses and donkeys, dogs, pigs, ducks--anything you could possibly want. How about it?"

Chot Caniet once more said, "Beat, friends, beat," and the beating stopped. So the monkey started to bring forth gongs, pens of buffalo, and rich houses plus every other imaginable thing. Chot Caniet saw that the houses were not usable, so he said, "Enough, enough," which the poles understood as their command to start beating the monkeys again.

"Wait!" the monkey cried. "Whatever you want, whatever there isn't enough of, I'll give it to you. Would you like a mattress for your bedroom? Or perhaps a new bedroom? It's yours."

"Beat, friends, beat" said Chot Caniet. And the beating stopped once more.

With all that the monkey gave him, Chot Caniet instantly became fabulously wealthy. He had fields and rice paddies and buffalo--as the saying goes, he had "a full house." His property and rice fields stretched as far as the eye could see in all directions, and a castle too.

"What shall I do now?" he thought. First, I must go get my wife. "Go to Aunt," he commanded his slaves, "and bring her here. She's living in a shack at that grassy place, and has only a few bowlfuls of rice left to eat. Take one of the vehicles and bring her here."

Soon the slaves arrived at Chot Caniet's shack at the edge of the jungle. "Uncle sent me for you, Aunt. He wants you to come home. Come home with me, Aunt."

But the wife was suspicious. "You're trying to get me to leave home, eh? In a little while Uncle will come home, and he'll scold me if I'm not here. His name is Chot Caniet, the one who always has a fever, who sleeps beside the ashes and was scalded with boiling water. You've come to get me, but I don't dare go. No, I won't go with you."

"If you don't leave, Aunt, Uncle will indeed scold you. You had better come pretty soon."

"No, you go on home. I'm not going with you. If Uncle returns, and there's nobody here, he'll really scold, believe me."

The slaves tried once more. "Please come. Uncle sent me to fetch you, because he isn't able to come himself. That's the truth. Please come."

"No, I won't go, and that's final. Please leave."

Seeing that it was pointless to try and persuade her further, the slave left and went back to the house of his master, who by this time had changed so that he was no longer itchy and scratchy. "Uncle, Uncle," he reported, "I told Aunt, but she refused to come."

"Why won't she come?" Chot Caniet asked.

"She said that she was afraid that you'd return and be very angry if she weren't there. She was afraid you'd think that she'd just gone off on her own, and later you'd return and beat her. It really is a pity. Your in-laws gave you presents and sent you on

your way; now, later, that you're all alone again, the one you
want to come join you is afraid to come."

"All right, children," replied Chot Caniet, "You stay home and
watch the house, and I'll go get her myself."

He changed himself once more back into his itchy and scratchy
form, and set off. Thump, thump, thump, went his walking stick as
he walked along back to his wife. He found her next to the cart,
right where he had left her that morning.

"So," his wife greeted him, "you've come home."

"Yes, but just a little while ago, I sent someone to get you."

"How was I to know that you were the one sending for me?"

Dropping that argument, Chot Caniet asked, "Have you cooked any
rice and soup yet?"

"I did cook some rice, but you didn't come home."

"Who wants that rice and soup, anyway? Let's go and eat at
home."

"Home? What are you talking about? Where do we have a house?"

"Come. I sent the servants to fetch you, but when you didn't
come, I came for you myself. Let's go home."

His wife still didn't understand, but she obeyed. They yoked
the buffalo, hitched them to the cart, and set off, with his wife
driving the cart just as before. Halfway there, Chot Caniet
magically changed his body again; his transformation made him
beautiful, like an angel. At that point, his wife began to understand. She stared, open-mouthed in amazement, at her husband,
previously so itchy and scratchy, now completely changed into
someone wonderful to behold. Then she noticed all the fields and
houses.

"Whose paddies are these? Whose rice fields?" she asked.

"They are ours," her husband replied.

"Whose house is that?" she continued, indicating a big, two-
storied tile house.

"It's ours," answered her husband.

"What about all of those others, those huge tiled houses over
there?"

"Those belong to all our friends, relatives, neighbors, and
officials."

Then they went up to the huge two-storied tile house that was
now their home, and Chot Caniet turned to his wife and said, "You
know what we'll do? We'll have a feast and invite our mother and

father. They took care of us, but now they have no idea how we are. They probably think we are dead. Let's have a feast and invite them."

"Go ahead," his wife assented.

So slaves were sent to deliver the invitation to the king: "In a few days, Father, we are going to have a feast. We would like you to come."

"What!" exclaimed the king. "Who is this Chot Caniet, anyway, that now he can invite me to a feast? It's been only a few days that I sent him out of here with a cart of rice and a pair of buffalo. How could he possibly have gotten ahead so fast? How could he possibly ever produce anything, being so itchy and scratchy?

"Well, if he really wants me to come, he can spread out a flowery mat from his house to mine. And give me a red horse. Yes, if there's a red horse, then I'll know I'm supposed to go." This was the king's way of saying that he wouldn't go to his son-in-law's feast.

"How could old Itchy-Scratchy produce anything worthwhile?" he kept thinking skeptically. "But, if he really wants me to go, he can spread out the flowered mat."

But Chot Caniet took his father-in-law at his word, and really did spread out a flowery mat, and even provided him a red horse! Clippity clop, cloppity clop, right down the mat pranced the red horse to the king's front door. The father-in-law couldn't get up on the horse, so instead he led it all the way to Chot Caniet's place. When he arrived, he saw how tremendously rich his son-in-law now was. And he saw that all of the important people were present: all of the chiefs, assistant chiefs, and other prominent people who had responded to Chot Caniet's invitation.

What a change had taken place! Previously his son-in-law had been all itchy and scratchy, but now he was perfectly all right. All of the people decided that now Chot Caniet should be their king. So from then on, the king rested, and let his son-in-law be king.

THE LAZIEST MAN IN THE WORLD

This story in Cua, as told by a seventy-year-old
grandmother and a fifty-year-old man,
was translated by Eva Burton.

Once there was a man named Sang Alah Kho Noiq. He was the laziest man in the world.

One day the family he worked for gave him the job of watching two buffalo. But Sang Alah Kho Noiq preferred sleeping to following the buffalo as they grazed. It was only a matter of time before one of the buffaloes wandered off and got lost. Sang Kho Noiq returned to his master with only one buffalo.

"Where is my other buffalo?" the owner cried. When he found out that the buffalo was lost, he demanded that Sang Kho Noiq pay him for the loss.

Sang Alah Kho Noiq didn't know what to do. He had neither family nor house, so how could he possibly pay his employer for the lost buffalo? Not seeing any solution to his problem, he lay down and slept so deeply, he looked like he was dead.

When the king of the ravens and his raven soldiers flew that way, they saw Sang Alah Kho Noiq lying there, and they thought he was dead. They flew down to have a look at him.

"His eyes look good," said the king. "I will eat them."

"His penis looks good," said the soldiers. "We will eat that."

Sang Alah Kho Noiq had heard every word the ravens said, but he feigned sleep. Just as the raven king was going to peck at his eyes, he reached out his hand and caught hold of the raven's leg. The raven king began immediately to beg and plead for mercy and forgiveness.

But Sang Kho Noiq replied, "I never threatened to eat you. You were the one who wanted to eat me. Why should I show you mercy? What will you give me if I forgive you?"

The ravens continued to cry out for mercy. Suddenly Sang Kho Noiq remembered that the ravens had a magic drum that could give one whatever he wished. He decided to demand that the ravens give him the drum.

So the raven king sent his soldiers to bring the drum from its hiding place by the seaside, and when they returned, he gave it over to Sang Kho Noiq.

Sang Kho Noiq beat on the drum and wished for a buffalo. Immediately a buffalo appeared. Now he would be able to pay for the buffalo he had lost! He beat the drum again, and food appeared, so he was satisfied. He forgave the raven king and let all the ravens fly away.

Then Sang Alah Kho Noiq went home and gave the buffalo to his master. He left home and wandered aimlessly about the countryside. Because of his magic drum he would never have to work again, he thought, so he just went wherever he felt like going.

At last he came to the foot of a **sung** tree and lay down to sleep. He just lay there for days, not going anywhere, not doing anything. Sang Alah Kho Noiq was the laziest man in the world. He never bathed; he never searched for vegetables or snails; he never got up for anything. If a fruit fell from the tree, right in his mouth, he ate it. If it fell beside him, he was too lazy to pick it up. Day after day, he just lay there.

One day a bird flew over the tree under which Sang Kho Noiq was sleeping. (It was either a raven or a magic bird; we don't know which.) The bird was carrying a fish in its mouth and dropped it right beside Sang Kho Noiq. The lazy man took the fish and filleted it, but he was too lazy to go to the stream right beside him to wash it. Instead, he urinated on it to wash it, then put it down next to him to dry. That's how lazy he was.

The next thing that happened was perhaps caused by the Sky, although it is not known for sure. In any case, a raven came along, saw the fish lying beside Sang Kho Noiq, picked it up in his beak, and flew off. As he flew over the king's palace, the raven dropped the fish, and it fell by the side of the king's well.

Perhaps it was the Sky that caused the next thing to happen as well. When the king's daughter came out to the well to play and get water, she noticed the fish and carried it into the house. Without washing it beforehand, she just fried and ate it. Sometime later she realized that she was pregnant.

When the king found that his daughter was pregnant, he asked her, "Who has been with you? Who have you slept with? Is he a man of importance, a rich man? Whose son is he?"

But his daughter answered, "No one. I haven't slept with anyone."

The king looked hard at his daughter and waited. But she was
able to look her father straight in the eye without being afraid
to speak to him, so nothing more was done.

In time the child was born. The king waited until he was about
three years old, and then he called all the province officials,
all the important people, and all the rich people to come to the
palace. Then he instructed his daughter's child to go around and
look carefully at everyone assembled there and pick out the one
who was his father.

The child scanned all the faces, but didn't see anyone who
might be his father, so he ran outside the gate to play. There he
saw Sang Alah Kho Noiq, leaning against the fence wearing only an
old g-string, barely enough to cover him. He had come only out of
idle curiosity. He wanted to know why the king had called together
all the important men in the realm.

Again the Sky intervened, and when the child saw Sang Kho Noiq,
he cried, "Father, Father!" Sang Kho Noiq had no idea why the
child was staring at him and calling him, "Father." He became
frightened, and started to run away. But when the king heard what
had happened, he sent out soldiers to capture the lazy man and
bring him to the palace.

When they arrived, the king began to question Sang Kho Noiq.
"When did you sleep with my daughter?" And, turning to his daughter, the king said, "So, you were sleeping with Sang Kho Noiq,
were you? Explain."

"I am the king's daughter," she replied. "Why would I take Sang
Kho Noiq, this poor ragged person, to sleep with? Even if I wanted
him, how would he ever know to come to my house?"

Then Sang Kho Noiq spoke up, "How would I dare to come to the
king's house? I am but a poor person. How would I dare to sleep
with the king's daughter in the palace of the king?"

The king refused to believe Sang's words. Instead, he became
very angry and "hot in his heart." He ordered his soldiers to cut
bamboo and make a raft. Then he took his daughter and her child,
along with Sang Alah Kho Noiq, down to the river. He made them get
on the raft and pushed them out toward the ocean to drown.

(Now the king's wife, who loved her daughter very much, had
taken a sack and filled it with husked rice. In the middle of the
sack, she had put a single piece of gold, then had given the sack
to her daughter before she got on the raft.)

Instead of going downstream to the ocean where they would
drown, the Sky caused the raft to go upstream to the place where

Sang Kho Noiq had left his magic drum. Sang took the drum, went off by himself to beat it, and wished for a little house for them to live in. Instantly a little house appeared, and there they took up residence.

Sang Kho Noiq continued to be very lazy and tired. One day his wife told him to stay home and watch the child and the chicken, while she went out to the field to work. As she left, she gave the child the piece of gold to play with.

So Sang stayed home, but he was too lazy to get up to do anything. When a chicken began to eat the husked rice, Sang was too lazy to get a stick and chase it away. Instead, he took the piece of gold and threw it at the chicken. The chicken pecked at the gold, and finally swallowed it.

When his wife came home and found that the chicken had eaten the gold, she was very angry. "All I have is my body to work, and one little piece of gold to keep us alive. Now you've lost the gold. What can you ever do to pay me back? This is more than I can bear! I won't stay with you any longer."

"Wait," Sang replied. "What do you want that you lack? You want your gold back? Let me teach you. Go out to the field."

So the woman, the cat, and the dog went back to the field. In the meantime, Sang Kho Noiq beat on his magic drum and wished for gold. When the woman reached the field, there smiling up at her, was a whole field of gold. She filled her basket with the gold and went back home.

Her husband saw the gold and asked, "Enough?"

"Enough," she replied.

Then Sang Kho Noiq beat his drum again, and soldiers appeared to work in the fields. He beat it again, and suddenly he had cows and buffalo. Soon he had everything he wanted, including a big house that was exactly the one his wife wanted.

Sang Kho Noiq ordered the soldiers to work the fields and tend the buffalo. But when they ploughed the fields, the river began to flood. It flooded until it came right up to the door of the king's palace.

The king saw the height of the river, and wondered, "What's happening? What is someone doing to the river to make it flood like this?" So he sent some of his soldiers and neighbors to find out what was causing the flooding. After traveling a long way, they came to the house of Sang Alah Kho Noiq beside the river. They saw how rich and powerful a man he was now. They noted the size of his house and the numbers of his soldiers and animals.

Then they went back to report to the king what they had seen. But the king was incredulous. "I myself put my daughter and Sang

Kho Noiq on a raft, and I saw it start drifting downstream toward the ocean. I know that they drowned."

No matter how many times the delegates repeated what they had seen, the king would not believe them.

Meanwhile, Sang Alah Kho Noiq said to those who came to look at his estate, "Would our mother and father like to come and visit us? Tell them they are welcome."

But when the king and his wife heard this they scoffed, "Oh, Sang Kho Noiq, who is he? Only a man with a ragged g-string. He is nothing. When he has gold doors and gold mats to sit on, then we will visit hm."

The people took this news back to Sang Kho Noiq. "Oh, so Mother and Father will come if I have gold doors!" he exclaimed. With a few beats of his drum, the door was covered with gold. He beat again, and three suns appeared on either side of the door.

Finally, the king and his wife did come to visit their daughter and Sang Kho Noiq. But when they arrived at the house and were greeted by the brilliance of the suns shining beside the golden door, they fell down in a faint. Sang Kho Noiq went slowly into the house, got his ragged g-string, waved it over them, in order to revive them.

Then they all went inside and ate together. After a bit, Sang Kho Noiq asked the king, "Why did you fall in a faint when you came to my door?"

"Never in all my life have I seen a house with a sun in front of it," the king replied. "When I saw yours, I fainted."

After the feast, Sang Kho Noiq ordered his soldiers to carry back gold as gifts to the king and his wife. From that day forward, the king and his wife did not dare to say anything disparaging to their children. And at last the king was truly happy.

THE LEGEND OF J'BONG ALAH

This story in Eastern Cham told by
Mr. Q., about forty-three years old,
was translated by Doris Blood.

Once upon a time, there was a very lazy fellow named J'Bong Alah. He didn't want to do anything except play around.

One day when some of the people were going out into the fields to catch fish, J'Bong's mother ordered him to go also, but he refused. She scolded him severely, but he still wouldn't go.

J'Bong left and went down the road where there was a mango tree loaded with fine fruit. He lay down under the tree and waited for a mango to fall into his mouth. He was too lazy to pick up one of the many mangoes that fell all around him.

After a while, the people who had gone fishing came along and saw all of the mangoes under the tree. When they started to gather them up, J'Bong stopped them. He told them that these were mangoes that he had picked himself, and that if they wanted some, they would have to barter with him. So they gave him some fish in exchange for the mangoes.

Then J'Bong took the fish and roasted them in the coals of a cremation fire. When he had roasted a spit of fish until it was well done, he would put it behind him and roast another. While he was busy, a ghost came along and snatched one whole spit. When J'Bong turned around, he noticed that one spit of fish was missing! He looked around to see who was responsible and caught the ghost in the act of stealing another spit. Quickly, he grabbed the ghost and held him by the beard. Threatening to beat or kill him, he demanded his fish back.

The ghost feared for his life, so he offered bribes of money, rice, gold, and silver. But lazy J'Bong was not interested. "I have plenty of money, rice, gold, and silver at home," he said. "Offer me something else."

94

"I'll give you a magic formula," the ghost said. "When you say 'jump,' people will jump; when you say 'stand,' they will stand still."

In exchange for this power, J'Bong let the ghost go free. When he went back home, he saw his mother weaving cloth. He ordered her to stop immediately and get some rice for him to eat. His mother merely scolded him severly for speaking to her that way.

"If you don't get some rice for me to eat," J'Bong warned, "I'll speak some magic words that will make you jump."

His mother continued to ignore his order, so he spoke the magic formula for 'jump.' Up jumped his mother with such force she wrecked the weaving loom. She jumped and jumped until she was worn out, and she begged her son, "Leave me alone, please, and I'll go get rice for you to eat. I'm afraid." So J'Bong spoke the magic words for his mother to stand still.

She went right away to get rice for him and carried it out in a pot, which she put in the middle of the yard. After J'Bong ate the rice, he put the pot lid on top of his head. Then he ordered his mother to go and ask the king to give him his youngest daughter in marriage. His mother said she wouldn't dare do any such thing.

"If you don't," her son threatened, "I'll make you jump again."

His mother was afraid of having to jump some more so she went off to the palace of the king. When she got to the outer gate, she dared go no further, so she just stood there. Her presence attracted the notice of the palace dogs, and they began to bark.

The king sent some of his servants to investigate the cause of the disturbance. They went out, saw the woman, and reported back to the king that J'Bong Alah's mother was standing outside the fence. The king then ordered them to go out and call her in.

When she had been brought before him, the king asked, "Where have you come from and what is the purpose of your journey?"

"Oh worthy king," she began, "I am the mother of J'Bong Alah, who ordered me to come and ask for your youngest daughter in marriage."

The king was so angered at this request that he took the mother, locked her up, and would not let her go home. Then he sent soldiers to arrest J'Bong and bring him back to the palace.

The soldiers found J'Bong still sitting in the middle of the yard eating rice, with the pot lid on his head. "Where have you come from?" he asked the soldiers.

"The king ordered us to come get you. You must come back with us to the palace where he can interrogate you. How dare you be bold enough to order your mother to go ask for the king's daughter?"

J'Bong replied, "Okay, if you want to take me go ahead." Then he spoke the magic formula, and all of the soldiers started jumping.

They jumped and jumped until they were exhausted. They began to stumble and fall, and they begged J'Bong to stop. "We won't dare to take you now! Enough!" So J'Bong again spoke the magic words, and the jumping ceased.

The soldiers went back to tell the king what had happened. They said that J'Bong was now a very powerful man. "He spoke a magic formula that made us jump until we were exhausted," they said. "We jumped so hard and so long, we almost broke our arms and legs. We don't dare go back to him again."

The king was furious. He ordered the soldiers to bring his sedan chair and convey him to the lazy man's house at once. Arriving at the house, he began to harang J'Bong: "How did you have the gall to order your mother to come and ask for my daughter? Now I've come myself to take you to the palace."

"Do you want to take me or not?" J'Bong challenged. The choice is yours. If you do, I'll speak the magic formula." And he did.

Immediately, the king jumped, falling from his hammock. All the soldiers jumped, too. Everyone jumped until they were exhausted, until their arms and legs were almost broken. Finally the king cried out, "Enough! I'm afraid of you now, J'Bong. I agree to give you my daughter in marriage." Then J'Bong spoke the formula, and everyone stood still.

The king climbed into his sedan chair and went home. J'Bong Alah followed along after him. At the palace the king called his youngest daughter to him, and said, "J'Bong Alah is now a powerful man. Agree to marry him!"

The princess obeyed her father, saying, "You have spoken, Father. Therefore, I agree to marry him."

Thus, the king let J'Bong Alah marry his youngest daughter and come to live in the palace.

'BOK 'BLAR (MR. LIAR)

This story was told in Rengao by a story-
teller from the village of Plei Jodrap,
and was translated by Marilyn Gregerson.

'Bok 'Blar[1] was faced with a problem--he had no wife. So he was trying to figure out how he could marry the rich man's daughter.

One night as he went out behind the rich man's house to relieve himself, he overheard the daughter talking with her father. Her father said, "Who do you want to get to help you in the fields? Be sure to choose someone who is healthy and strong and be sure that you don't marry a lazy man!"

That night 'Bok 'Blar laid awake thinking about what the rich man had said.

Before dawn the next morning, he said to his mother, "Mother, pound some rice."

"Why are you telling me to pound rice?" she said. "You never get up this early!"

"Please pound rice and cook me some rice and vegetables," he replied. "I want to go out to the fields early this morning when the other villagers go out to work."

As soon as he had eaten, he grabbed his bushhook and his hoe and ran off to join the other villagers who were leaving to go to the fields.

When the other villagers saw 'Bok 'Blar, they asked, "Why are you going with us? You haven't even planted a field!"

"Oh, I just decided to go out and work today," he replied.

"Alright then, I suppose you can come along with us," the villagers answered.

When they got to the fields, 'Bok 'Blar worked as hard as he could. He found a place to work near the rich man's daughter and worked hard all day long.

When she got home that night, her father asked her, "Who helped you in the fields today?"

"'Bok 'Blar did," she answered; "He really worked very, very hard."

But her father found that hard to believe; he thought she must be lying.

The next morning 'Bok 'Blar went out again and worked as hard as he could all day long helping the rich man's daughter. When she got home, her father asked her again, "Say, daughter, who helped you work today?"

"Well, 'Bok 'Blar helped me," she answered. But the rich man wouldn't believe her.

The next day the rich man secretly followed the workers out to the field. From his hiding place he saw for himself that 'Bok 'Blar was really working hard--in fact, harder than anyone else. "He's the one my daughter will marry. He'll be my son-in-law," he said to himself.

The next morning, the rich man told his daughter, "Go call Grandfather Bogap." So she did as she was told and went to call Bogap.

"What's this all about?" Grandfather Bogap said.

"Who knows? Come and find out," she replied. So Bogap went over to see the rich man.

"Mr. Rich Man, what did you call me for?" asked Bogap.

"I want you to go ask 'Bok 'Blar if he would like to marry my daughter."

"You must be joking!" laughed Bogap.

"No, I'm not. I want him to marry her," said the rich man. So Bogap went over to see 'Bok 'Blar. "The rich man wants me to find out if you're interested in marrying his daughter," he said.

"Oh, you must be joking, Uncle. I'm such a lazy person. My father and mother are very poor; we don't even have a decent house--not even any fields! How could I marry the daughter of a fabulously rich man?"

"Oh, that's no problem. The rich man insists that he wants you to marry her," replied Bogap.

"Well, if he insists, what can I say? Sure, I'll marry her," answered 'Bok 'Blar.

Bogap went back to the rich man and said, "'Bok 'Blar says he wouldn't have the audacity to even think of marrying your daughter. He doesn't have any possessions, and besides that, he's very poor and lazy."

"So what if he's poor, I know that," responded the rich man; "so what if he's lazy, I know that. If I want him to marry my daughter, he'll marry her."

"Alright, if that's what you want," replied Bogap. So they talked back and forth and completed the first stages of the marriage.

Then the day came to celebrate the final stages of the wedding. The rich man beat the drums and called all of the villagers together, "Go out and gather greens. Today my daughter will celebrate her wedding." So off they went to gather greens.

The following day, the young unmarried men got the wine ready. Then they called the rich man's daughter and 'Bok 'Blar. They all ate and drank their fill and everyone enjoyed a bountiful feast.

About three months later, the rich man went out to check his fields and saw the tracks of a wild boar that had been eating his rice. He went home and said to his daughter, "Daughter, tell your husband to stay out in the field tonight and keep an eye on it. If the wild boars eat our rice, then what will we eat?"

That afternoon the rich man's daughter said to 'Bok 'Blar, "My father wants you to go out and sleep in the fields. He's afraid the wild boars will eat the rice."

"What's this?" responded 'Bok 'Blar. "I told you before that I'm not brave, not at all brave. I'm a coward, a real coward. Now he insists on telling me to go stay out in the fields."

"What's the difference," she said, "whether or not you're brave. There are the two of us."

"What, could you go?" scoffed 'Bok 'Blar. "No, just let me go alone."

His wife handed him his sword, but he didn't want it. He just took his bush hook and an old torn blanket, and off he went to the field.

There he was out in the field feeling miserable; he didn't have anything to eat and he was scared to death. He decided to climb a tree and stay high up in its branches. So he stayed up there and slept.

All at once 'Bok 'Blar heard a tiger roar. The tiger got closer and closer and closer. He was in such a fright that he defecated all over his loincloth and all over his blanket.

When it was almost morning, the tiger, while jumping up trying to get 'Bok 'Blar, got his paw caught in a branch. As the sun came up, 'Bok 'Blar looked down and saw that the tiger was stuck fast in the branch and couldn't free himself. So he climbed down and hurried home.

He said to his wife, "Last night, I couldn't sleep because I was so afraid."

"What were you afraid of?" she asked.

"Well, I'll make no secret of it. If I hadn't been so brave and clever, a tiger would have eaten me up."

"Where did this happen?" she asked.

"Out there in the field. Here your father tells me to go out and watch the field, and I almost get eaten by a tiger!"

"I think you're lying." she replied.

"What do you mean, lying?" he said.

So she went to her father, "Say, Father, 'Bok 'Blar says that he has captured a tiger and put it up in a tree out in the field."

"Oh, he's lying, Daughter," laughed the rice man.

"Well, okay, but why don't you go check it out?" she said.

So the rich man and all the villagers went out to the field. Some carried crossbows, some carried swords, others carried knives and bush hooks.

When they got to the field they were amazed to see that indeed there was the tiger hanging in a tree. No matter how hard the tiger tried, he couldn't get himself loose. So they shot him with crossbows and killed him. When they got closer to the tiger, however, they smelled feces. "Why does this tiger have feces on it?" they asked.

"Well, when I climbed up, I defecated on his head," responded 'Bok 'Blar. So they took the tiger and washed it and then roasted it and ate it.

Well, things went on normally for some time. Then one day a stranger from another village arrived in the rich man's village. He told them that his village was continually plagued by seven tigers that had eaten all their cattle and water buffalo and were now on the verge of eating people, too.

The stranger said, "'Bok 'Blar, we won't beat around the bush. We want you to come and help us. We are desperate to get rid of these seven tigers who have been eating up our cattle. If you don't come and help us, how will we be able to live? We'll pay you generously for your help."

"How could I do that?" replied 'Bok 'Blar. "I'm a coward. I'm not brave."

"Oh, yeah," replied the stranger, "we know that you're a coward and not brave at all! Please say that you captured a tiger and stuck him up in a tree! So please agree to come and help us."

"Well, okay, then I'll come with you." said 'Bok 'Blar.

His wife handed him his sword to which he responded, "What will I do with that? My bush hook is good enough." So he followed the stranger to his village.

As they were approaching the village, 'Bok 'Blar said to his companion, "Go on ahead; I want to stop and relieve myself." So he squatted down near a rattan clump.

Just then he saw a tiger coming towards him. "What are you doing, 'Bok 'Blar?" the tiger asked.

"Well, I've come out here to get some rattan," answered 'Bok 'Blar.

"What will you do with the rattan?" asked the tiger.

"I want to tie my wife and children to the house. If I don't tie them down, the big storm that is coming will flood the earth and they will be washed away. Take a look at the sky how it is shaking and vibrating."

The tiger looked up at the sky and saw the clouds moving. "Say, you're right. We're in a real bind, aren't we? Say, 'Bok 'Blar, would you tie us down?" asked the tiger.

"Well, how can I do that? I already have plenty to do. Oh, okay, I guess I can help you if you will go and pull out some vines."

So the seven tigers went over to the mountain and pulled out some big jungle vines and brought them back to 'Bok 'Blar.

"Now tie us down," they pleaded.

So 'Bok 'Blar tied the seven tigers to an enormous tree. On and on he worked while the storm was brewing. Finally, they were tied up from head to foot.

"Now look, you try to squirm real hard, okay? Then I'll whip you to see if I've tied you good enough," said 'Bok 'Blar.

"What do you mean, whip us?" roared the tigers.

"Well, if I don't whip you, you might come loose and be blown away in the storm."

"Okay, go ahead and whip us," they answered.

So 'Bok 'Blar cut a whip of bamboo and whipped the daylights out of the tigers. They writhed and squirmed, but they couldn't get loose.

"Okay, you all wait here," said 'Bok 'Blar, and he walked into the village.

"Where have you been so long, 'Bok 'Blar?" the villagers asked.

"Why wouldn't I be gone for quite a while? I did have to tie up the tigers over there," 'Bok 'Blar replied.

The villagers took their shields and swords and ran out into the forest. When they got to the tree, all they could see were tiger stripes all over the place. They took their swords and crossbows and shot all of the tigers. When the tigers were all dead, 'Bok 'Blar and the villagers went back to the village.

"Alright now, anyone who has possessions must give half of them to 'Bok 'Blar," the elders declared. So the villagers divided up all their possessions and gave half of everything to 'Bok 'Blar: half of their slaves, half of their buffalo, cattle, pigs, and chickens--half of everything they had. Then they helped 'Bok 'Blar carry all his possessions back to his own village.

When they arrived at the rich man's house, the rich man slapped his thigh. He was happy that his son-in-law was so smart. After that, 'Bok 'Blar never did any work. All he did was eat and sleep and get up. He never went to work in the fields at all.

Then, after some time had passed, one day his father-in-law went out to inspect his fields. There he saw some elephant tracks. "If the elephants eat our rice, what will become of us?" he asked himself.

So back home he went and said to his daughter, "Daughter, go tell your husband to go and sleep out in the field. The elephants are eating up our rice."

So the daughter went to tell 'Bok 'Blar, "My father wants us to go out to the fields and keep watch for elephants because they have been eating up the rice."

"This is the sort of thing I never liked," he said. "I'm a coward and I'm afraid. I didn't want to marry you because of this, but your father insisted. But finally he said, "Well, I guess there is no other alternative. If we die, we die. If we live, we live."

So he took his crossbow and his sword and off they went to the fields. After they got there, they cooked rice and ate. Then 'Bok 'Blar went to sleep and his wife kept watch.

After dark 'Bok 'Blar's wife heard the rumble of elephants coming toward the field. They got closer and closer. She tried to wake 'Bok 'Blar, but he pretended to be fast asleep. Actually, he defecated in his loincloth because he was so scared.

Since she couldn't get a rise out of 'Bok 'Blar, she grabbed the crossbow and began shooting at the elephant. The elephant ran off, but when it got to the edge of the field, it collapsed and died. The next morning very early, 'Bok 'Blar got up. He went to the edge of the field and saw the carcass of the elephant. Then he cut up a large tree and made a big trap. When the trap was finished, he tied the elephant's leg to it so it would look like it had been snared in the trap.

When his wife woke up, he said to her, "Who told you to shoot the elephant?"

"Well, if I hadn't, he would have trampled us," she replied.

"Why did you have to go and shoot the elephant? I wanted him alive; instead you have killed him!"

"Well, how was I to know?" she answered, "You didn't say anything about a trap."

"Well, okay, but don't cut up my elephant to roast him. Just leave him lying there where he is," he said.

After they returned to the village, 'Bok 'Blar's wife told her father, "Father, we shot an elephant, but 'Bok 'Blar won't let anyone roast and eat it. He says he wants to leave it right there at the edge of the field."

"Well, whatever he says is okay," responded her father.

So they just let the elephant lie there and rot. Finally, one day 'Bok 'Blar went out to the field and saw that there were some vultures going in and out of the rotting carcass eating the innards. 'Bok 'Blar watched from a hiding place and when most of them were inside, he ran out of his hiding place and plugged up the anus of the elephant. By that time, it was late afternoon. Then 'Bok 'Blar said to his wife, "Go ahead and climb up on the elephant." So she did as she was bid, and they both climbed on the elephant. Then he took a switch and whipped the elephant. This made the vultures fly around and flap their wings furiously inside the elephant. Then 'Bok 'Blar and his wife flew over to the village and landed right beside the rich man's house.

Well, the rich man was really happy now. He had a son-in-law who had a flying elephant! He was really proud of this son-in-law of his.

One day a couple of months later, 'Bok 'Blar said, "Say, why don't we fly the elephant over to Laos and see if the King of Laos wants to buy it?"

So they flew over to Laos and landed right next to the palace. The King of Laos greeted him and asked him what he was doing.

"I won't beat around the bush. I came to see if you wanted to buy my flying elephant."

After the king's son saw that it could really fly, he said to his father, "Oh Dad, buy it! Buy it, Dad! If you don't buy it, I'll just die."

The king said, "Well, wait until tomorrow and we'll see." So they prepared wine, killed chicken, and feasted.

"How much do you want for your elephant, Friend?" the king asked.

"Just a hundred slaves, a hundred head of cattle, a hundred elephants, a hundred pigs, a hundred chickens, a hundred wine jars, a hundred iron kettles--just a hundred of each, that's all."

So the Laotians rounded up all the things he had asked for and asked him to check them over. 'Bok 'Blar's list took nearly everything the king owned. After he had turned it all over to the new owner, 'Bok 'Blar said, "Now look, later on, don't come to me complaining about anything, okay?"

"What's there to complain about?" replied the king. "Go ahead and take your stuff home.

Now 'Bok 'Blar was really rich and his father-in-law was ecstatically happy. The two of them just sat around and feasted all of the time.

Meanwhile, back in Laos, the king's son said to his father one day, "Let's go and visit our friend out east, okay?" So they got on their elephant and off they flew. As they were flying over the ocean, the king's son said, "Say, Dad, I have to defecate."

"Go ahead," his father answered. So the son defecated on the back of the elephant.

"What will I use to scrape this off, Dad?" the son asked. "Oh, I'll pull out this stick and use that."

So he pulled the stick out of the elephant's anus to scrape off the excrement. Then the vultures inside saw the light and immediately flew out one by one. Now the elephant, empty of vultures, fell down into the ocean, and the King of Laos and his son drowned.

But back in his village, 'Bok 'Blar just lay around all the time in his house. Then there was another rich man from a distant village who had heard how rich 'Bok 'Blar was. "Let's go and attack 'Bok 'Blar," he suggested to his friends. "You five guys go first."

So off the five men went. When they got to 'Bok 'Blar's house, they called out, "Is anyone home?"

"Sure, we're home," 'Bok 'Blar's wife answered, even though 'Bok 'Blar was out. So they came up to the house and she served them food.

"Where are you all going?" she asked.

"Well, we'll get right to the point. The rich man in our village heard that 'Bok 'Blar is fearless, so we want to challenge
him to a fight. If he wins, he takes all of our stuff. If we win,
we take all his stuff.

"When do you want to fight him?" she asked.

"At full moon," they replied, "under the big ironwood tree over
there."

When 'Bok 'Blar came home that evening, his wife told him about
the visitors.

"What's this? I'll be killed for sure. I'm just one, and there
are many of them. What will I do now?" Finally, he said "Well, if
I die, I die, and if I live, I live."

When the day of the full moon came, 'Bok 'Blar took his shield
and sword and went off in the direction of the big ironwood tree.
He climbed up the ironwood tree and made himself a platform high
up in the branches. When the moon came out, he heard voices below.
There were scads of men down there--maybe hundreds, even thousands
of men. He heard them say, "Why should we be afraid of 'Bok 'Blar?
He's just one man, and there are a lot of us. We'll chop him up in
little pieces and carry off his wife."

They sat under the ironwood tree for a long time and waited for
'Bok 'Blar. "Why hasn't he come yet?" they asked. "Well, we might
as well go ahead and eat." So they started to prepare their food.
They caught fish and frogs and put them in bamboo to cook. As they
were eating their food, 'Bok 'Blar was up in the tree getting more
frightened by the minute. He was so frightened he started to
defecate. Some of the feces fell into one of the men's bowls. That
man said to the man next to him, "Hey, what do you mean by
throwing this crap in my food?" Before the man could answer, the
first man grabbed his sword and killed the one he thought had done
it. Then the dead man's son said, "Why did you kill my father?"
and he grabbed his sword and killed his father's murderer. Then
another man said, "Why did you kill my mother's younger brother?"
and he killed his uncle's murderer. Still another man said, "Why
did you kill my father's younger brother?" and he killed his
uncle's murderer. In response another man said, "Why did you kill
my parent's older brother?" and so he killed that murderer. And so
it went on and on until everyone was dead except for five men.

Then 'Bok 'Blar called down to them, "Wait right there. I'm
coming down." Those five men, assuming 'Bok 'Blar to have killed
all the men lying around, when they saw him, were so terrified
that they ran off in all directions.

Then 'Bok 'Blar came down from the tree and gathered up some of
their clothes, shields, and swords and took them to his house.
Then he made two platforms for two of their elephants to transport

the rest of his newly acquired possessions and drove their
elephants and cattle back to his house.

The rich man was overjoyed that his son-in-law was so smart and
so brave. He killed a buffalo and a cow and had his slaves prepare
a feast.

From then on, the rich man and 'Bok 'Blar just sat around and
supervised their slaves.

NOTES

1 'Bok 'Blar literally means 'Grandfather Liar.'
2 Gogap literally means 'one who joins together.'

Publications of the
INTERNATIONAL MUSEUM OF CULTURES

1. SARAYACU QUICHUA POTTERY by Patricia Kelley and Carolyn Orr, 1976.
   (Also available in Spanish as CERAMICA QUICHUA DE SARAYACU) $ 3.00

2. A LOOK AT LATIN AMERICAN LIFESTYLES by Marvin Mayers, 1976. $ 6.45

3. COGNITIVE STUDIES OF SOUTHERN MESOAMERICA by Helen Neuenswander
   and Dean Arnold, eds., 1977. (Also available in Spanish as
   ESTUDIOS COGNITIVOS DEL SUR DE MESOAMERICA.) $10.95

4. THE DRAMA OF LIFE: GUAMBIANO LIFE CYCLE CUSTOMS by Judith Branks
   and Juan Bautista Sánchez, 1978. $ 5.00

5. THE USARUFAS AND THEIR MUSIC by Vida Chenoweth, 1979. $14.95

6. NOTES FROM INDOCHINA: ON ETHNIC MINORITY CULTURES by Marilyn
   Gregerson and Dorothy Thomas, eds., 1980. $ 9.45

7. THE DENI OF WESTERN BRAZIL: A STUDY OF SOCIOPOLITICAL ORGANIZATION
   AND COMMUNITY DEVELOPMENT by Gordon Koop and Sherwood G. Lingen-
   felter, 1980. (Also available in Portuguese as OS DENI DO BRASIL
   OCIDENTAL--UM ESTUDO DE ORGANIZACAO SOCIOPOLITICA E DESENVOLVIMENTO
   COMUNITARIO.) $ 6.00

8. A LOOK AT FILIPINO LIFESTYLES by Marvin Mayers, 1980. $ 8.45

9. NUEVO DESTINO: THE LIFE STORY OF A SHIPIBO BILINGUAL EDUCATOR
   by Lucille Eakin, 1980. $ 2.95

10. A MIXTEC LIME OVEN by Kenneth L. Pike, 1980. $ 1.50

11. PROTO OTOMANGUEAN KINSHIP by William R. Merrifield, 1981.
    (Also available in Spanish as PARENTESCO PROTO OTOMANGUE.) $12.00

13. STICKS AND STRAW: COMPARATIVE HOUSE FORMS IN SOUTHERN SUDAN
    AND NORTHERN KENYA by Jonathan E. Arensen, 1983. $12.00

14. GRAFTING OLD ROOTSTOCK by Philip A. Noss, ed. 1982. $10.95

15. A VIEW FROM THE ISLANDS: THE SAMAL OF TAWI-TAWI by Karen J.
    Allison, 1984. $ 6.90

16. YAGUA MYTHOLOGY: EPIC TENDENCIES IN A NEW WORLD MYTHOLOGY
    by Paul Powlison, 1985. $12.00

17. GODS, HEROES, KINSMEN: ETHNOGRAPHIC STUDIES FROM IRIAN JAYA,
    INDONESIA by William R. Merrifield, Marilyn Gregerson,
    and Daniel C. Ajamiseba, eds. 1983. $15.00

18. SOUTH AMERICAN KINSHIP: EIGHT KINSHIP SYSTEMS FROM IRIAN JAYA,
    INDONESIA by William R. Merrifield, ed. 1985. $12.00

19. FIVE AMAZONIAN STUDIES ON WORLD VIEW AND CULTURAL CHANGE by
    William R. Merrifield, ed. 1985. $11.00

20. THE FORMAL CONTENT OF ETHNOGRAPHY by Philip K. Bock, 1986. $9.50

21. TALES FROM INDOCHINA, by Marilyn Gregerson, Dorothy Thomas,
    Doris Blood, and Carol Zylstra, eds. $11.00

These titles are available at

The International Museum of Cultures
7500 W. Camp Wisdom Road
Dallas, Texas 75236